Praise for *Painless Performa*

D0362053

"In this field-tested work, you will learn tips, tools, and techniques to help make the entire process of performance conversations a far more pleasant one for all concerned. It's a highly readable work and a must-read for all supervisors and managers."

—**Edward E. Scannell, CMP, CSP**
Coauthor, *Games Trainers Play* series;
McGraw-Hill, Past National President;
ASTD, IFTDO, MPI and NSA

"Marnie Green has a talent for presenting complicated, abstract ideas in a simple, no-nonsense way that is easy to apply. Her tips for establishing performance expectations and for initiating the toughest conversations take the pain out of these critical tasks."

—**Kevin Klimas**
President and Founder, Clarifacts, Inc.

"This book should be required reading for all managers. Those who follow the painless approach will have high-performing employees and enhanced organizational performance."

—**Neil E. Reichenberg**
Executive Director, International Public
Management Association for
Human Resources

"*Painless Performance Conversations* is a painless read. It actually was just plain fun! It will inspire you and others to try new techniques for working with your most valued resource—your people. *Painless Performance Conversations* is a winner!"

—**Karen Thoreson**
President, Alliance for Innovation

"This book reflects Marnie Green's can-do attitude and offers step-by-step methods to which many will turn repeatedly as they meet the challenges of supervising others."

—Christine Kajikawa Wilkinson
Senior Vice President, Secretary, and
President of the Alumni Association,
Arizona State University

"Marnie Green has helped the city of Las Vegas with leadership development for over a decade. Our employees are better off as a result of Marnie's advice on how to handle performance conversations."

—Elizabeth N. Fretwell
City Manager, City of Las Vegas

"In her latest book, Marnie Green walks you through the steps to becoming your own expert on conducting performance conversations. Her practical counsel, exceptional writing style, and insight from years of coaching leaders make this a must-read book."

—Richard S Deems, PhD
President, WorkLife Design;
Coauthor of *Leading in Tough Times,* on Microsoft's and
Eaton's Recommended Reading Lists;
Author of *Interviewing: More Than a Gut Feeling*

Painless
PERFORMANCE
CONVERSATIONS

Painless PERFORMANCE CONVERSATIONS

A Practical Approach to Critical
Day-to-Day Workplace Discussions

MARNIE E. GREEN

WILEY

Library of Congress Cataloging-in-Publication Data:
Green, Marnie E.
   Painless Performance Conversations: A Practical Approach to Critical Day-to-Day Workplace Discussions/Marnie Green.
      pages cm.
   Includes index.
   ISBN: 978-1-118-53353-6 (pbk.); ISBN:978-1-118-63159-1 (ebk);
   ISBN: 978-1-118-63170-6 (ebk); 978-1-118-63181-2 (ebk)
 1.   Communication in personnel management. 2.   Employees–Rating of. I.   Title.
   HF5549.5.C6G73 2013
   658.3'125–dc23   2012047253

Printed in the United States of America

10 9 8 7 6 5 4 3 2 1

For Steve, with whom conversations are always painless

Contents

Preface

Have you ever faced an employee issue that you would rather avoid? If so, this book is for you. *Painless Performance Conversations* deals with the hard stuff that comes with being a manager, which is why it has been a long time in the making. It sprang from consulting and coaching work that I've done over the years with hundreds of managers who struggle with the day-to-day conversations they need to have with their employees. In workshops and webinars based on my first book, *Painless Performance Evaluations: A Practical Approach to Managing Day-to-Day Employee Performance,* I saw that managers always seemed to understand the need to lead an annual performance evaluation conversation. They even recognize the importance of documenting performance examples throughout the year. The angst appears, however, when the manager has to talk with the employee about not meeting performance expectations. The face-to-face, heart-to-heart discussion can turn the most seasoned, robust manager into a wimp.

Painless Performance Conversations is written to give you the boost you need to tackle the conversations you'd rather avoid. There's no shame here. Regardless of your position within the organization and the number of years you've been managing, delivering the news that an employee is not stacking up can be tough. But it doesn't have to be.

Conversations are living and breathing events with a multitude of moving parts. Psychology, emotion, experience, perspective, and perceptions: they all affect the outcome of performance-related conversations. Much has been researched and written about how our brains function when we have to engage in conversations about potentially unpleasant topics. This book takes the next step and gives you the tools you need to stay focused and feel confident when your brain is telling you to otherwise avoid the conversation.

The Pain in Performance Conversations

So what makes certain performance-related conversations painful when others are not? Several elements are usually in play to create the pain, and they all come down to fear. Fear of the unknown, fear of losing control, and fear of failure all compel us to avoid the conversations that are critical to our operations. And, on top of it all, the conversation is usually with a person with whom you would like to have a positive relationship. It's more pleasant to work with others when there is an absence of conflict. So you avoid the important performance-related conversations in an effort to avoid stress.

The conversation may be painful because you are unclear about how the interaction will end. As the boss, you are used to having the answers. When you enter into a conversation with an employee about his or her performance, you may think you know exactly what the employee needs to do differently. However, the employee will have his or her own ideas, and this difference of perspective can be threatening, especially when you are used to being in control.

When it comes down to it, performance conversations are painful because you make them so. When you worry about losing control, your focus shifts away from the ultimate outcome: improved performance. Painful conversations become painless when the conversation is focused on helping the employee be successful in your organization. We all want to be successful, and that requires feedback.

At the basic level, all humans crave interaction and feedback; without it we cannot succeed. In the work environment, employees need, want, and expect your attention and insights. It is your job and your responsibility to provide employees with the time and attention they need to be able to meet the job's performance expectations. Yet a number of factors, such as a lack of time or confidence, get in the way of carrying out this essential duty.

After using the *Painless Performance Evaluation* framework for a number of years to help managers turn the performance evaluation process into a productive one, it became evident to me that the next step was to focus on developing tools and approaches that would make managers fearless in leading the challenging day-to-day conversations. Once you have the tools and the perspectives of painless performance conversations, you will have the confidence to be an effective manager.

Performance Conversation Tools

Throughout this book you'll find a variety of tools that will make mastering performance conversations a snap. Watch for the following features in each chapter to guide your way:

- *Painless Perspectives:* summary thoughts that reinforce a key principle of painless performance conversations

- *Reflection Questions:* questions to encourage consideration of each concept as it applies to your own situation
- *Let's Apply It:* application exercises to link the concepts to real-life situations
- *Conversation Checkpoints:* summary ideas from each chapter
- *From the Field:* cases studies or reports from real-life managers who are using the painless performance conversations principles

What This Book Is and Is Not

Let's be clear about the scope of this book. Managers have performance conversations every minute, every day, throughout the year. Performance conversations span the lifecycle of each employee, as illustrated in Figure I.1. Conversations are necessary when the employee is new to the organization, when performance expectations change, when the annual performance

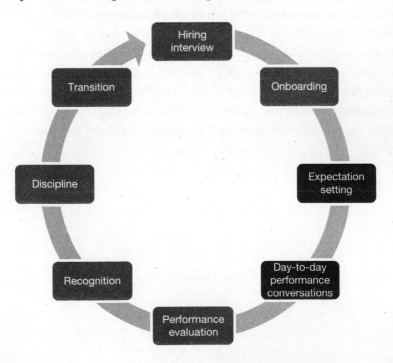

Figure P.1 Performance Conversations Throughout the Life of an Employee

evaluation is due, and when there are problems in the employee's performance that require corrective action. They offer an opportunity to provide positive feedback on a job well done and are critical to acknowledging and supporting the employee's contributions.

These conversations may run from easy to painfully difficult depending on the employee's performance and your relationship to the person. The focus of this book is not about new employee onboarding meetings, and it is not about discipline and corrective action. It will not address having performance evaluation meetings. You can find that information in *Painless Performance Evaluations: A Practical Approach to Managing Day-to-Day Employee Performance*. This book also does not dive deep into the importance of documenting the results of your performance conversations, although that is a critical step in the overall management of employee performance.

Instead, this book will guide you through the critical skills and tools you need to tackle those regular, everyday, normal conversations that spring up in the workplace and cause you to take pause. Painless performance conversations are the ones you know you need to have, and the ones you usually have an excuse for putting off. They are the discussions that let employees know how they are doing, that refocus employees when they are heading down the wrong paths, and encourage employees to try something new because they are currently not as effective as they could be. In this book you will learn a painless approach to potentially painful conversations so that you can give employees the communication and feedback they crave and deserve.

Painlessly yours,
Marnie E. Green

Acknowledgments

You don't write a book like this alone. Many people have helped develop these concepts and field test them in real-life situations. In every workshop I facilitate, in every conference presentation I make, and in every coaching conversation I have, the principles of painless performance conversations have been formulated, tested, and revised. So for the individuals I'm unable to name here, please know that I appreciate the influence you have had on the development of this work.

I extend my thanks to Matt Holt and Shannon Vargo at John Wiley & Sons, Inc., for believing in this project and for helping me make it way better than where we started. Many thanks also go out to fellow authors and cheerleaders Ed Scannell and Dr. Richard Deems, who showed only enthusiasm for my efforts. You two are icons in my book.

Jolaine Jackson, human resources extraordinaire and owner of On the Spot Resources, served as an essential resource to me in the development of the concepts and in the organization of the chapters. Jo, you got me jump-started when I was ready to forget about it.

Nancy Van Pelt, Tracy Bannon, and Kay Wilkinson generously read drafts of the manuscript and used their coaching and human resources expertise to fine-tune the language and the focus. You guys served as my reality check, and I'm appreciative of your candor.

My dear friend and hiking partner, Dr. Michelle May never stops believing in me and what I can achieve. Your subtle and not-so-subtle nudges kept me moving forward toward the completion of this book. I wonder what you'll encourage me to try next?

Everyone deserves a Jenniffer in their life. My long-time executive assistant Jenniffer Jarvis keeps me sane, makes me look good, and is always excited to take on the new and challenging projects I dream up. This book and my work would not be possible without her creativity, loyalty, and enthusiasm. Are you ready for the next big challenge, Jen?

Over the past few years, a slew of clients and colleagues have shared with me their painful performance conversation stories. Each chapter of this book includes one of their case studies. In particular, thank you to the following people for taking the time to write a case example upon which I could further develop: Cheryl Cepelak, Mike Sung, Kay Wilkinson, Jeff Knapp, Mark Olson, Debbie Kent, Rick Hunt, Jay Somerville, Roy Sugimoto, Stephen Cleveland, Jess Campbell, Ann Roseberry, Tamara Becker, Vicki Grove, and Jay Castellano.

I offer my deepest gratitude and love to my parents, who never doubt my abilities. You gave me the best foundation upon which to build this wonderful life I'm living. Finally, it is truly a wonderful life when you get to share it with your best friend, confidante, and soul mate. Thank you, Steve, for putting up with my hours in front of the computer and days on the road. I can't imagine anyone else with whom I'd rather share this adventure.

1

Be a Catalyst

Fostering Painless Performance Conversations

One person can be a change catalyst, a "transformer," in any situation, in any organization.

–Stephen R. Covey

Employees initially come to work for a paycheck, but few stick around just for the money. In a survey conducted by the Society for Human Resource Management, 53 percent of employees listed pay as a very important aspect of their job satisfaction. At the same time, more than half said relationships with an immediate supervisor were a critical factor in their job satisfaction. Studies have repeatedly shown that employee satisfaction is directly linked to employees' relationships with their immediate managers. As a manager, you have a direct impact on employee retention and engagement, workplace morale, and organizational culture.

An important part of your job as a manager is to tap into the passion that brings employees to work each day. When those passions are engaged and employees feel valued, they are likely to perform at higher levels. One reason employees stick with an employer, and with you as their manager, is the feeling of being valued. Employees are eager for your feedback, and your job as a manager is to provide them the reinforcement they crave.

But let's be realistic. You also have a really heavy workload. You are constantly juggling your focus between your own work and your employees' needs. As a result, it's easy to lose sight of one of the most critical roles that *you* play: a catalyst, someone who drives initiatives forward and provides a spark for change, serving as an igniter of passion. Catalysts help *others* take on more responsibility, rather than taking it on themselves. When you act as a catalyst, you help others function independently and confidently so that you can focus on moving the work group's and the organization's goals forward.

As a manager, you wear many hats, including technical expert, budget balancer, customer service champion, organizer of the work, scheduler of assignments, conflict resolver, problem solver, coach, mentor, and cheer-leader of employees. At times, you play the role of counselor. At other times, you take on the job of mediator or facilitator.

Painless Perspective

As a manager, your first job is to be a catalyst, a spark for change.

However, the most powerful role you can play is that of a catalyst. As a catalyst manager you inspire, excite, and nurture an engaged work culture. You use your influence as a catalyst manager to create a positive environment

Table 1.1   Catalyst Manager versus Typical Manager

Typical Manager	Catalyst Manager
Maintains status quo	Seeks new and better results
Gets work done	Creates new opportunities
Completes defined goals	Establishes new and challenging goals
Preserves	Promotes
Sustains performance	Takes performance to the next level
Reinforces accepted ideas	Provokes new thinking

where each individual excels to the best of his or her ability. When you think of yourself as a catalyst, you become a more effective manager. Table 1.1 lists some distinctions between typical managers and catalyst managers.

The Primary Tool of Catalyst Managers

Being a catalyst for action and change requires you to take on some difficult tasks, such as defining your performance expectations clearly for your employees. Catalyst managers challenge the status quo regularly, and this task is next to impossible if your employees are not on board. Most important, catalyst managers have frequent, meaningful conversations to influence performance. Any one conversation has the potential to shift an employee's perspective, to influence that person's choices, or to affect his or her performance.

Have you ever avoided a conversation with an employee about something because you were uncomfortable bringing it up? Customer service issues, attendance, hygiene, poor work quality, lack of teamwork . . . each situation calls for the conversations you should be having, rather than avoiding. As a catalyst manager you can use conversations to shift the status quo.

Painless Perspective

As a manager you automatically have an impact on others. The nature of your impact is up to you. Be a catalyst.

Employees Want Meaningful Conversations

The research organization *Leadership I.Q.* found that 66 percent of employees said that they have too little interaction with their bosses. Sixty-seven percent of employees said they get too little positive feedback from their bosses. In summary, roughly two-thirds of the workforce says they want more quality interactions with you. They want to know more about what you're thinking, and they want to know how they're doing.

It's clear that employees want meaningful two-way conversations that help them be successful. They want to know that they are adding value to the organization and that their passions and efforts are recognized and appreciated.

Specifically, employees want from you:

- A vision for how their work fits into the big picture
- Your time and attention
- Feedback that will help them improve
- Recognition of their efforts

Painless Perspective

Employees need and want your perspective so that they can be successful.

Painless Performance Conversations Defined

This book will help you learn to lead even the most difficult performance conversations with confidence. Regardless of the subject, or the seriousness of the issue, performance conversations can be painless for both you and the employee. This book will show you how.

The definition of a *painless performance conversation* is that it is a conversation with a *person you care about* concerning an *issue you are concerned with* where the *outcome is uncertain* and the *situation requires your influence.*

Let's break down the definition to explore what this really means:

1. *You care about the person.* In the workplace, the people you care about are those who are important to your success and to the success of the organization. You have a performance conversation because you care about the other person professionally. You care about his or her success because it leads to *your* success as a manager, which ultimately leads to the success of your organization. You may not be friends, and you don't really have to like the employee. You do, however, care about the employee professionally, or there would be no need for the conversation. Because you are in a professional relationship with the employee, you care.

2. *You are concerned about the issue.* Performance conversations help you accomplish your goals and support larger initiatives. Whether you are focusing on your organization's broader mission or your individual goals, conversations drive initiatives forward. Painless performance conversations are those where the issue cannot be ignored and a resolution needs to be found. As a catalyst manager, you use conversations to drive these issues forward. Your effectiveness in leading conversations about employee successes and failures will ultimately determine your own effectiveness, value, and promotability in your organization.

> *You want people walking away from the conversation with some kernel of wisdom or some kind of impact.*
>
> —Harry Dean Stanton

3. *The outcome is uncertain.* When the outcome of the conversation could go in multiple directions, the uncertainty makes the situation uncomfortable. Likewise, when the solution to the problem is not evident or when you don't know how the employee is going to react, the conversation has the potential to be painful. Painless performance conversations typically begin with an uncertain outcome, but you pursue them because something needs to change.

4. *The situation requires your influence.* You wouldn't be thinking about having the conversation if something hadn't caught your attention. Whether it is output that is not up to quality standards or team member interactions that are not positive, if something isn't right in the workplace, you have the ability to have an impact on the issue. Speaking up with the intent to sway, disturb, or alter the status quo is the job of a catalyst manager. Painless performance conversations are ones in which your influence will ultimately have a positive impact on the behavior of others.

Ultimately, painless performance conversations are those that cause employees to make a shift. They have a tremendous impact on a work group because they allow everyone to move forward. The affect of any one conversation may initially be small, but no matter the immediate outcome of a performance conversation, every conversation will have an influence. Be a catalyst.

Subjects of Painless Performance Conversations

Painless performance conversations can relate to any workplace issue, including those that begin like this:

- "We've received customer complaints about your work."
- "Your response to that customer complaint created additional problems for our team."
- "Your colleagues have complained about an offensive odor coming from your cubicle."
- "You are not meeting your production quotas."
- "You have contributed to the team producing results at levels that are lower than we've seen in the past two years."
- "You have shown a pattern of tardiness."
- "The records indicate that you have been using your cell phone and computer for personal business."
- "We needed your assistance, and we couldn't locate you for 2 hours."

Reflection Question

What performance conversation do you need to have with an employee right now?

Avoiding Performance Conversations

Painless performance conversations are the day in and day out, formal and informal exchanges that you have with employees that help them meet or exceed your expectations. Most of these conversations are already painless, and you tackle them with ease. The potentially painful conversations are usually preceded with thoughts like:

- "If I don't mention this issue, maybe it will go away."
- "I don't have time to deal with this right now."
- "I think I'll just wait and see what happens."

You may be tempted to avoid certain performance conversations. However, the impact of not taking action can have tremendous consequences, including:

- Nothing changes!
- The problem gets worse.
- Customer service suffers.
- Team morale is negatively affected.
- You lose credibility up and down the chain of command because problems are being ignored.
- The employee's behavior may negatively affect others on the team.
- Important changes may not be implemented.
- Lack of conversation stunts the professional growth of you and the employee.
- Avoidance creates an appearance of favoritism.
- You or others experience increased stress.
- The employee's workload may shift to others, creating inequities.
- The employee's or coworker's physical safety could become jeopardized.
- A legal liability may be created.

If those reasons are not enough to convince you to address performance issues immediately, consider the financial impact on your organization if employees were more productive—even if by only 1 percent. Imagine your payroll costs are $1 million a year and you improve employee performance through conversation by just 1 percent. The bottom line impact would be at least $10,000. What could you do with an additional $10,000 in your budget? If employees are less productive than they could be, what is the cost to your organization and to you as a manager?

Let's Apply It

Complete the form describing a performance-related conversation you need to have with an employee. The conversation can be about anything related to improving an employee's performance.

Your Performance-Related Conversation

With whom do you need to have a performance conversation?	What issue(s) need to be addressed?	What is the impact to you if you do not have this performance conversation?	What is the impact on your organization if you do not have this performance conversation?	What is the impact to the employee if you do not have this performance conversation?

As you continue to read *Painless Performance Conversations,* refer back to this personal example to assess your readiness for the conversation. In the upcoming chapters, you will learn concepts and tools that will help you to more clearly frame and address your situation.

Painless Performance Conversations and Painless Performance Evaluations

The job of managing employee performance is not a one-step task. It is the ongoing and continual responsibility of every manager. Performance conversations are a critical element in the larger process of performance management. How you handle them will determine whether they are painful or painless.

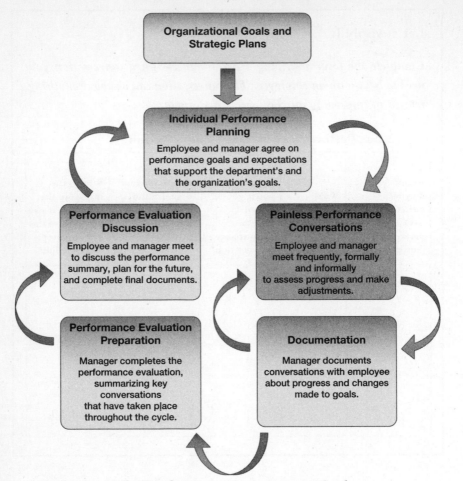

Figure 1.1   The Performance Management Cycle

Typically, performance evaluations are completed once per year or on some other interval determined by your organization. Well structured, they are based on predetermined criteria or expectations that are usually linked to job performance standards or organizational objectives. Performance evaluations are best prepared as a summary of the conversations you and the employee have had throughout the year. The performance management cycle illustrates this concept (Figure 1.1).

Performance conversations are not a replacement for a performance evaluation, and the performance evaluation is not a substitute for regular performance conversations. Regular performance conversations, adequately documented, make it easy to have a painless performance evaluation because the end-of-the-year conversation is a summary of the previous conversations and the employee isn't surprised by its content.

What's Ahead?

Although many books and references have been developed to guide managers through difficult conversations, the painless approach is simple. The first step is to set clear expectations that define success. Chapters 2 through 4 will give you the tools you need to define your expectations and then convey them in a way employees understand and support. In Chapters 5 through 8, you will explore the four mind-sets required to confidently master performance conversations with employees:

- Lead with Behavior: Separating Actions from Attitudes
- Eliminate Judgment: Focusing on Performance Evidence
- Inquire with Purpose: Using Curiosity to Expand Possibilities
- Be Clear: Creating a Culture of Ownership

Once you have mastered the mind-sets necessary for a painless performance conversation, Chapter 9 will offer you the best approach for initiating the conversation, following a simple road map to keep you from getting sidetracked. Finally, Chapter 10 illustrates specific performance conversations you may encounter.

Conversation Checkpoints

- As a manager, you are the catalyst for change in your organization.
- Employees want to have conversations with you. Foster an environment that is open to painless performance conversations. Initiate them.
- Avoiding a performance conversation will affect you, the employee, and the organization.
- Performance management is a continual process.
- Performance conversations are the link between day-to-day performance and the performance evaluation.

From the Field

From Bill, City Manager:

I hired a manager who had great recommendations and a strong reputation as a leader in his field. The new manager got off to a strong start by hiring staff and developing a project plan for the team to follow. Along the way, however, the manager ignored important procedures and created conflicts with managers in other departments. He occasionally threw his own team members under the bus if they were not "in line" with his vision.

I had plenty of excuses for not addressing the manager's performance sooner. Other issues distracted me. I gave the manager the benefit of the doubt based on his reputation and recommendations. I let the issue go on for too long.

When I finally took time to check in with the team, I learned that the new manager was making their lives miserable. Several high-potential team members quit before I was able to address the issue. I had done too little, too late.

In the end, I learned that it was my job to stay connected with the performance of the entire team, as well as with the performance of the managers I relied upon. Having regular conversations with the manager about his team and its progress would have given me the opportunity to deal with these issues before they became nearly impossible to resolve.

Sound Bites from the Field

If Bill had initiated a conversation with the manager sooner, it may have started like this:

I noticed that the reconciliation process that the team has developed was not followed last month. I also heard that you and David had a heated argument about the Williamson project on which both of your teams are working. These two issues concern me. What happened?

Just initiating conversations about these issues and others would have opened the door to a dialogue with the manager about his approach. Bill may have been able to head off some of the problems the team faced had he engaged in these conversations sooner.

Lessons Learned from the Field

Bill learned a costly lesson when he allowed the new manager to do whatever it took to the get the job done. By not initiating performance conversations as the issues arose, Bill:

- Lost good staff
- Lost productivity
- Increased the cost of the operation
- Lost revenue
- Decreased employee morale

Along the way, Bill probably lost the respect of others in his organization who were affected by the new manager's ineffectiveness. Only Bill could influence the situation, and eventually he realized his ability to be a catalyst for change. It's never too late to begin addressing performance issues through conversation.

Next Up

In Chapter 2 you'll explore what may prevent you from initiating performance conversations, and you'll learn how to differentiate between your personal pet peeves and true performance issues.

2

Have the Guts

Tackling Performance Conversations Head On

By "guts" I mean grace under pressure.

—Ernest Hemingway

What workplace conversations give you the willies? Which employee discussions would you rather avoid? With the job of management comes the task of addressing problems or tough issues, even though you'd rather not have to handle them. You procrastinate. You hold out for what you think is the right time. You wait to see if the problem will take care of itself. You avoid the issue. In most cases, the waiting only makes the situation more challenging, which makes the eventual conversation more painful.

You may put off certain conversations because you don't know exactly what you want to say. Often procrastination is caused by an inability to pinpoint the real issue. You know you are not satisfied with the status quo, yet you struggle to articulate the issue without making it emotional.

Regardless of how the prospect of the conversation makes you feel, performance-related conversations are your job as a manager. Every conversation you encounter with employees will shift the organizational culture and influence how employees perform. If you don't address issues that affect productivity and morale, who will? One of your many roles as a manager is to have the so-called tough conversations. Your day-to-day conversations, easy and difficult, guide your work group and help your organization function effectively.

The first step is to embrace this responsibility and stop putting off the hard work. Management takes courage. It takes guts. It takes nerve to quell a performance crisis that is generated by an underperforming employee; it may also be the most important action you perform (or don't perform) as a manager. It is your job.

Painless Perspective

Employee performance problems rarely, if ever, resolve themselves! It is up to *you* to take action!

You're an Avoider If . . .

You know you are avoiding an important performance conversation if:

1. You are afraid of what might happen if you raise the issue.
2. You secretly hope the issue will just go away.

3. You think you don't have time to have the conversation.

4. You don't really know how to go about having the conversation.

5. You know the employee is going through stuff and you don't want to add to his or her stress.

6. You don't enjoy having performance conversations with employees.

7. You think the employee is a nice person and you don't want to hurt him or her.

8. You believe the message can be more effectively delivered via e-mail.

9. You begin to avoid the employee altogether to ensure a conversation opportunity doesn't present itself.

10. Your fear keeps you from acting.

These are common avoidance tactics, and they will prevent you from being a catalyst manager and affect the success of your work group.

Let's Apply It

Place a checkmark next to any of the following statements that have crossed your mind when facing the prospect of a performance conversation.

☐ It's uncomfortable.

☐ I hope the problem will fix itself.

☐ The problem is so obvious, the employee should know better.

☐ I don't like drama.

☐ I'm uncertain about how the employee will react.

☐ I just don't want to do this.

☐ Different employee personalities make it hard.

☐ I didn't see the employee do it myself. I've only heard rumors.

☐ I'm busy and don't have time to have lengthy conversations with employees.

☐ The employee is *so* good in other areas of their job; I don't want to jeopardize the good performance.

☐ Someone else in the organization is telling me the issue is no big deal.

☐ I'm concerned that my peers and/or my boss won't support me.

☐ Having the conversation might jeopardize my friendship with the employee.

☐ Team morale may be affected.

☐ I might hurt the employee's feelings.

☐ I'm worried the employee might clam up.

☐ I'm concerned the employee might show aggression.

☐ I'm afraid the conversation might make the employee's performance worse.

☐ The employee might cry.

☐ I don't want to hear the employee's excuses.

☐ I'm afraid I can't clearly describe the issue in the performance documentation.

☐ It may create more work for me in the long run.

☐ It's embarrassing for the employee to talk about.

☐ It's embarrassing for me to raise the issue.

☐ It's hard to explain the issue in a way the employee will understand.

Consider the responses that you checked and ask yourself whether your reaction is a valid reason for putting off the conversation.

Reflection Questions

What performance conversations have you avoided in the past and why? What performance conversations are you avoiding right now? What's stopping you?

Embrace It

To be an effective performance manager, you have to embrace your role as a catalyst. In this role, you assume the responsibility to guide your employees toward the organization's goals. You take on the responsibility to provide timely and constructive feedback. You own the responsibility to be honest with employees about how their work is affecting the group.

Embracing your role as a catalyst manager takes guts and focus. Talking with employees about challenges, problems, and failures is often unpleasant. However, it comes with the job of a manager. Having guts to manage means you embrace the responsibility to be honest, consistent, and fair with your feedback.

Likewise, embracing your role as a catalyst means you take full responsibility for the outcomes. Blaming your boss, other people, or policies for not having the conversation only deflects the responsibility that comes with the job. Think about a problem you and your team have faced lately. Did you search to blame someone for the outcome? Did you use external factors that were out of your control as an excuse for subpar performance? Ideally, you used conversation to explore what you and the team could do to positively influence the situation. Embracing your role as a catalyst means that you are constantly looking to resolve issues through conversation, rather than finding excuses for why you and the team can't perform.

There are many ways of allowing your thinking to get in the way of your performance and learning, but they all amount to conversations you are having with yourself within your own head.

—Timothy Gallwey

The Potentially Long Road

On one hand, having a difficult conversation with an employee often results in a sense of relief. It feels as if you can finally check a big item off of your list. You can now move on to the next item on the agenda, right? Not so fast!

Unfortunately, one conversation is rarely the end of the issue. Frequent conversations are part of the continual performance management process. As a manager you must be prepared to have performance-related conversations every day with employees, keeping in mind that conversations are not conducted in a vacuum. A series of conversations might be required to influence the behavior of an individual employee or to affect the overall performance of your team. For example, if the purpose of the conversation is to redirect an employee's efforts, you will need to have a follow-up conversation to recognize improvement or provide further correction. If the employee does not improve, you will need to have a conversation again to redirect the employee's efforts. These performance conversations might be repeated multiple times before you see improvement. And, if the conversations don't result in improved performance, you will need to take progressively stronger steps to influence the behavior you expect.

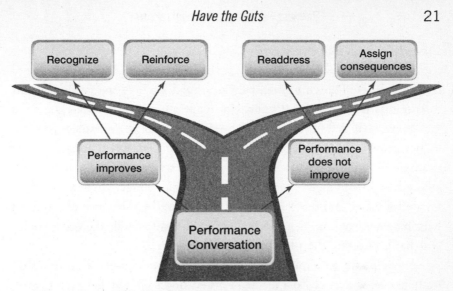

Figure 2.1   The Performance Conversation Journey

When embarking on a performance conversation, remember that the first conversation won't be the last. In fact, you may be embarking on a journey that looks like that shown in Figure 2.1.

Finally, as you consider whether it's time for a performance conversation with an employee, ask yourself if you are mentally prepared to go down the road. The road may be bumpy and full of potholes, yet the conversation journey is the only path to performance improvement. It is a road you must go down.

In a perfect world, the road is short and leads to immediate improvement. The employee hears your message and makes the necessary adjustments. However, in certain cases, the road will be a long one if improvement is not made. If you work in a large corporation, a unionized environment, or a public agency where employees have extensive due process rights, the road may be lengthy and arduous. The road will take you to unpleasant destinations such as discipline hearings, mediation, and possibly a courtroom. On this road, your actions as manager will be tested and questioned.

Painless Perspective

Knowing the performance management road will be a long and challenging one, prepare yourself for the journey.

Deciding to Take the Road

Before you begin down a potentially long road, there is one more question to consider. Is the employee's behavior really a performance issue, or is it a pet peeve that is bothering you? Sometimes the performance you are focusing on may not be directly related to the work environment. For example, if you are bothered when employees talk over the water cooler about the previous night's game, yet they are able to meet your expectations for performance and serve customers as expected, your concern may be a personal one. You may be the one who has the issue, while the water cooler chitchat is boosting the morale of the employees.

A pet peeve is a minor annoyance that you identify as particularly bothersome, to a greater degree, than others find it. We all have pet peeves. But when does a pet peeve become a legitimate performance issue?

Ask yourself: "Is this issue affecting the employee's ability to meet the established performance expectations? Does it impact his or her ability to provide the service that's expected?" If your answer is "yes," proceed with the performance conversation. If your answer is "no," you have likely uncovered a pet peeve. Asking these questions first, before addressing the concern with the employee, will provide you with the confidence and clarity to proceed.

Here are a few potential pet peeves expressed by managers compared with their potential impact on the workplace:

Manager's Pet Peeve	Potential Impact on the Workplace
Employee is too chatty.	Employee disrupts coworkers and the team is not meeting goals.
Employee pretends to be too busy to help a customer or answer the phone.	Customers are not being served.
Employee gives me the silent treatment for days after we have a disagreement.	There is no impact unless avoiding you affects the employee's ability to accomplish work or effectively support the team.
Employee looks bored while working at a public service desk.	This is not a performance issue unless the employee's expression affects customer satisfaction or outcomes.

(*continued*)

Manager's Pet Peeve	Potential Impact on the Workplace
Employee chews gum too loudly.	This is not an issue unless it becomes a distraction for others.
Employee leaves the lights on after exiting an empty room.	This may not be an issue unless there is a clear expectation to conserve energy.
Employee does not make a new pot of coffee after taking the last cup.	This is probably not an issue unless it is indicative of other behaviors that show a lack of teamwork and regard for others.
Employee talks too loudly on the phone.	Employee disrupts coworkers and distracts others.

The key is to determine how the employee's behaviors are affecting others in the workplace or customers. If there is no direct impact on the work environment, on the organization's image, or on the employee's ability to produce results, the issue is your pet peeve. Any of the aforementioned behaviors may be considered a legitimate performance issue, depending on how it affects the employee's ability to contribute.

Reflection Questions

What are your pet peeves? What do employees do that drive you crazy?

Pet Peeve Formula

To determine whether an issue is your own pet peeve or a true performance issue, ask yourself:

- What exactly is the **behavior** that is not meeting my expectations?
- How does the behavior **affect** the work environment, the organizational culture, others' work performance, or the employee's ability to meet job expectations?
- What behavior do I **expect** to see instead?

It's easy to be distracted by your own personal irritations. When the behavior that is bothering you affects the employee's ability to be effective or affects others in the work environment, it is worth a conversation. If it doesn't affect the work environment, let it go.

To clarify this further, here are a few examples that illustrate the difference between a pet peeve and a legitimate performance issue.

> *Manager complaint*: "It bothers me when employees don't stay current with e-mail and other communications."

Begin with the three questions in the Pet Peeve Formula:

1. *What exactly is the **behavior** that is not meeting my expectations?* Not responding to e-mails is clearly an observable behavior. You can see when an e-mail was sent and when and how it was responded to. You can compare the e-mail time and date to your expected response. In addition, there may be an organizational policy or expectation that defines how quickly e-mails are to be responded to.

2. *How does the behavior **affect** the work environment, the organizational culture, others' work performance, or the employee's ability to meet job expectations?* When an employee does not return e-mails or phone calls promptly, depending on the job, it can have a significant impact on the work environment because unanswered e-mails usually mean someone's request or question has not been addressed. Responsiveness is an indicator of professionalism and customer service. Unreturned or delayed responsiveness can mean lost or disappointed customers. It can also mean that others are not able to move ahead with their work.

3. *What behavior do I **expect** to see instead?* The behavior you expect is a response within a certain time frame, which may reflect an organizational expectation. For example, the expectation might be that all e-mails are returned within 24 hours of receipt.

Not responding to e-mails or phone calls in the expected time frame is clearly a job-related, observable behavior. It's not a pet peeve. It requires a painless performance conversation.

> *Manager complaint*: "My gripe is people who are just too chatty. I encourage a positive work environment, but telling an employee that we have heard enough about her child's accomplishments is difficult."

Begin with the three questions in the Pet Peeve Formula:

1. *What exactly is the **behavior** that is not meeting my expectations?* When the conversation is not work related, it can take valuable time away from the day. Identify what is not getting done or how customers are affected by the employee's lack of focus. The behavior itself may not be the problem; however, if work suffers because of the behavior, it is worth addressing.

2. *How does the behavior **affect** the work environment, the organizational culture, others' work performance, or the employee's ability to meet job expectations?* If an employee is unfocused and spending time talking about non-work-related issues, it may mean that critical work is not getting done. What is not getting done? What is not getting the attention it deserves? If the chatty employee is getting his or her work done, how are others affected by the employee's behaviors?

3. *What behavior do I **expect** to see instead?* Rather than telling the employee that he or she should stop talking, focus on what you expect the employee to do instead. It could be that you expect a higher level of production, a faster response rate, or higher levels of productivity from the entire team.

The chatty employee can have a positive impact on the work environment—boosting morale and building team spirit. If this is the case, addressing the employee's behaviors and expecting a change may not be productive. However, when the employee's enthusiasm impedes his or her own or other's ability to focus on the job at hand, it's worth a conversation.

Manager complaint: "The employee chews gum too loudly."

Begin with the three questions in the Pet Peeve Formula:

1. *What exactly is the **behavior** that is not meeting my expectations?* The employee is chewing gum loudly.

2. *How does the behavior **affect** the work environment, the organizational culture, others' work performance, or the employee's ability to meet job expectations?* The answer to this question depends on the nature of the work and whether others have complained about the employee's gum chewing. If the employee does not interface directly with customers and others have not complained about the gum chewing, the gum chewing is not affecting the work environment. If that's the case, it is your own pet peeve.

3. *What behavior do I **expect** to see?* When the issue does not affect the work environment and you've determined that it is a pet peeve, a conversation is not required.

Chewing gum in many workplaces is considered unprofessional behavior. However, your job as a manager is to assess the impact of the gum chewing on the environment before addressing it as a performance issue. If there is no effect on workplace, this may be an issue better left alone.

Let's Apply It

Describe the last time an employee did not perform up to your expectations. Apply the Pet Peeve Formula to your situation to determine whether the issue was a pet peeve or a legitimate concern by asking yourself:

- What exactly is the **behavior** that did not meet my expectations?
- How does the behavior **affect** the work environment, the organizational culture, others' work performance, or the employee's ability to meet job expectations?
- What behavior did I **expect** to see instead?

Creating a Clone or a Valued Contributor

When your goals for addressing a performance issue are clear, you will be able to more effectively influence the behavior of the employee. Before you initiate a conversation with an employee about performance, consider your ultimate goal. What are you trying to achieve from the conversation? Ask yourself:

Am I trying to make the employee think and act like me?

or

Am I encouraging the employee to think independently and create innovative solutions?

In other words,

Am I trying to create a clone, or am I trying to develop a valued contributor?

Here are some critical differences:

Clone	Valued Contributor
Follows procedures	Focuses on results
Asks for specific answers	Explores possibilities and options
Meets the minimum	Seeks to excel
Complies	Creates
Raises concerns	Provides options
Viewed as a cost	Viewed as an asset
Lays low	Catches the eye of management
Reads directions	Learns or creates new ways
Focuses on the job assigned	Thinks about the big picture
Plays it safe	Takes calculated risks

Managing employee performance means you are leveraging your resources. If you could do it all yourself, you would. But you can't. It is critical to develop trust with the employees with whom you work. Allow them to excel. As a manager, your employees' success makes you look good. Employees are contributors, and you need everyone's contribution to reach your organization's goals.

Conversation Checkpoints

- Avoiding a performance conversation can make the situation worse. Embrace your responsibility to address issues as soon as possible.
- Performance conversations are rarely a one-and-done proposition. They have to be repeated to have a lasting impact.
- Taking on an employee performance issue may mean you will have to commit to traveling a long road to resolution.
- Before starting a performance conversation, determine whether the issue is a pet peeve or an issue that affects the work environment.

From the Field

From Lydia, Attorney:

When I am out of the office I expect my assistant to "handle things." That's what I pay her for. Often if I've been out of the office for a few hours, I return to a stack of phone messages and notes that require my response. I've told my assistant time and again that she is to take care of the details of the office so that I can concentrate on the legal work.

I was so frustrated recently when I returned from a meeting to find a stack of messages and documents that I had not expected. Rather than say something, I decided to just suck it up and just get the work done.

My rationale for not having the conversation seems logical. I don't want to strain my relationship with my assistant. She is an important part of my success, and I don't want to hurt her feelings. I am afraid that if I bring up the fact that she isn't handling things while I am out of the office, she will get defensive and cry. It feels easier to just return the calls and do the work myself.

However, I realize that if I continue to respond this way, my assistant will continue to repeat the same behaviors. Things will never change. I am going to ask my assistant to help me understand how she decides which calls require me to call them back and which ones she can handle on her own.

Sound Bites from the Field

The conversation between Lydia and her assistant began like this:

Lydia: You are an important key to the success of this office. The more details you handle, the more I can focus on securing new clients and delivering service. Can we talk about some ways you can help me focus on those activities?

Assistant: Sure.

Lydia: I noticed that when I'm out of the office, you are diligent about taking phone messages. I appreciate that. Some of those messages are easy to reply to, and others are more complex. I would like to see you handle more of the calls while I'm out of the office. The more calls you can resolve, the more time I have to focus on our clients' larger concerns.

Assistant: But I'm worried that I might not answer their questions correctly. I don't want to create more problems for you.

Lydia: I know you are concerned about accuracy. At the same time, there are many calls that I know you can resolve immediately. Can we take a look at some of the most recent calls you've received and begin to identify which issues you can resolve on your own?

Assistant: I guess so.

Lydia learned that the assistant did not feel like it was her place to speak on Lydia's behalf. To help her feel more confident, Lydia asked her to create a list of commonly asked questions, including what she thought the answers would be. They went over the scenarios together and developed a framework to use when Lydia was out of the office. Once it was clear that Lydia expected the assistant to respond to the routine questions, the assistant began resolving more of the routine issues herself. Lydia can now focus on the bigger issues of the day. Once Lydia spent a little time laying the groundwork, the assistant's confidence grew. They spend a little time each week to go over new issues and questions. The assistant's focus is now on making Lydia's job easier and on eliminating intrusions so that Lydia can focus on the legal side of the house and not on the routine matters.

Lessons Learned from the Field

Lydia learned that when she didn't take the time to explain her expectations to the employee, she couldn't expect the employee to meet or exceed those expectations. Employees are not mind readers. Lydia assumed the employee knew that she was expected to respond to all of the phone calls. She thought the employee knew what she meant by *handle things*. Lydia realized that the performance issue she thought was the employee's problem was really a problem to which she had contributed.

Next Up

In Chapter 3 you'll identify the performance expectations you have for employees, and you'll learn a simple tool for defining and clarifying those expectations. You'll also explore how to manage your expectations, especially in the midst of rapid change.

3 | Form Clear Expectations

Making Your List

We tend to get what we expect.

—Norman Vincent Peale

Employees are not mind readers. So why do managers often say:

"The employee really should know that. He's been through training."

"Everybody knows that's not appropriate or acceptable."

"Isn't that just common sense?"

"Everybody else can do it without hand holding. Why can't she?"

"Doesn't everyone know they are supposed to be courteous and accurate?"

What if all you had to do was imagine a job well done and employees would carry out the work just as you have imagined? Unfortunately, it doesn't work like that. If you were promoted up the ranks and came into the job of management with experience and expertise related to the job you are now managing, it's easy to see the technical solutions. You know exactly what your success tools are. Your employees, however, may not have the same experience with the work as you do. Now, instead of doing the tasks, your job is to convey clear expectations and help employees achieve them. Essentially, your new success tool is to be clear and specific about what you expect.

All managers hope that employees understand the basic tenets of good, professional work. However, what good looks like to you may be very different from what the employee thinks is good. What may be taboo in your work unit may have been standard practice in the employee's previous experience.

For employees to be successful, your number one job must be to help your employees see your expectations as clearly as you see them. The first step in achieving this is to define what success looks like. Once you've done that, you can then clearly convey your expectations. This chapter focuses on the first step: how to define your performance expectations.

If you don't know what you expect, you can't be clear with employees about what success looks like. Being clear about your expectations is not as easy as it sounds. It requires continually being in communication with your team. But you have countless conversation opportunities in the course of your day to set expectations, revise your expectations, and clarify your expectations. These everyday conversations will help you develop positive rapport with employees, which makes performance conversations painless. Let's explore some tools for getting clear about your expectations.

Clear Expectations

You've probably experienced this common yet frustrating conversation pattern with an employee:

You: I need you to complete the reports and file them on time. Do you understand?

Employee: Yes. *(with a head nod)*

What the employee produces is something less than you envisioned. The reports were not complete, were not accurate, and/or were not on time. Yet, the employee indicated that he knew exactly what you were asking for. It's easy to have a picture in your mind of the end result, while the employee has a different image.

Painless Perspective

Never ask, "Do you understand?" The answer will be "yes" 99.99 percent of the time, and you rarely get a clear perspective of what the employee understands.

For example, if you picture a chair in your mind, you might envision a recliner in your living room or an Adirondack chair on the porch. If you asked your employee to picture a chair, he might picture a rocking chair in his child's nursery or a beach chair on his favorite expanse of sand. Everyone's image will vary to some extent. It's easy to conjure up an expectation, but expressing it to others as you see it is a larger challenge. The expectations in your mind are meaningless if the employee doesn't see the same picture. Clear expectations allow employees to feel confident about the work they are about to accomplish.

Sources of Expectations

Job-related expectations can come from a variety of sources. Some expectations for employees are established by your organization. Many other expectations are set by you, the manager.

Organizational Expectations

Many of the expectations you have of employees come from organizational policies, norms, and traditions. These are expectations that you probably didn't craft on your own as a manager. However, they are expectations that you must be familiar with, support, and apply.

For example, organizational expectations come from:

- Job descriptions
- Organizational values
- Company mission
- Procedure manuals
- Desk manuals
- Employee handbooks
- Human resources policies
- Standard operating procedures
- Your boss's priorities (whether or not you personally agree with them)

As a manager, you will share and reinforce these organization-wide expectations with employees often. Thus, it's critical that you be knowledgeable of them so that you can guide employees appropriately.

Your Personal Expectations

As a manager, you bring a set of perspectives and priorities that are valuable to the organization. You have your own expectations about how employees should perform their work, what good work looks like, and what the end product should be. These ideas must be clearly shared with employees as part of your ongoing performance conversations. They must also be linked to outcomes that are important to the work group and the organization; otherwise, your expectations are just pet peeves.

Your personal expectations establish the culture of your work group. These expectations convey to employees how to behave day in and day out, and they define the principles by which work gets done. Because conveying your expectations is the most influential tool you have to affect the culture of your work group, the remainder of this chapter focuses on tools you can use to define your own performance expectations.

In the role of manager, your team is watching you. They are trying to figure out who you are and what you expect. The team is seeking to understand how they can be successful under your leadership. If you are a new manager and you haven't been clear about your expectations, start now. Take time today to clarify what you expect and share your ideas with your staff. The clearer your expectations, the more likely your employees will be able to meet them.

The greater danger for most of us lies not in setting our aim so high that we miss it, but in setting our aim so low that we reach it.

—Michelangelo

Determining Your Personal Expectations

Coming up with expectations that reflect success for your work group will take some thought. Here are four steps for thinking through your personal performance expectations:

1. Take time to think about what is most important to you in the workplace. Ask yourself questions such as:
   a. What does great performance look like to you?
   b. If you expect employees to be prepared, what does that look like in this work group?
   c. If you expect accuracy, what does that mean in this group? What is your margin for error?
   d. How do you expect the team members to relate to one another?
2. Write a list of expectations that define great performance. Brainstorm any and all ideas, as you will edit your list and revise it before finalizing it for your team.
3. Once you think you have a good list, share it in a staff meeting or during informal conversations with employees. Ask them to add to your list and provide you with feedback. Ask them what they think great work looks like.
4. With your employees' input, revise the list and use it to provide day-to-day feedback to your team and to orient new employees to the work unit.

The list becomes a template around which you lead the day-to-day painless performance conversations with your employees. It becomes the baseline against which you measure performance, and it sets the bar for how employees are expected to behave every day.

Reflection Questions

How do your employees know what is important to you? Do you have a written list of expectations?

Creating Your List

As you draft your list of expectations, keep the following guidelines in mind. Clearly stated expectations:

- Describe what you expect employees will do, rather than what you don't want them to do.
- Reflect critical behaviors of successful employees.
- Contribute to team and organizational success.
- Reflect current priorities of the work group.
- Help employees understand why things are done the way they are.
- Provide a link to overall company goals, showing how the group's work fits into the bigger picture.
- Apply the expectations consistently to all team members.
- Allow employees to explore alternative approaches while providing the guidelines to help them be successful.

Here is an example of one manager's list of expectations for an office receptionist:

- Arrive to every meeting on time or early.
- Always bring the necessary information and tools to each meeting (paper, pen, agenda, and working documents).
- Always leave a current voicemail message on your phone.
- Return every phone call within 24 hours of receipt.

- Acknowledge each walk-in customer within 15 seconds.

- Ensure no surprises between yourself, your teammates, and your manager by alerting the team of pending issues or potential roadblocks.

Notice this list of general expectations is not a list of job duties or performance goals. The list describes what is important to you as a manager and allows you to explain the nonnegotiable behaviors you expect in the workplace. It doesn't include deliverables or tasks you expect the employee to complete. Those expectations are conveyed using other tools, such as performance plans and job descriptions.

The list will vary based on the nature of the work environment. For example, if you work in a shop or a production facility, you may have specific expectations related to safety. If you work in customer service, you may have expectations related to how quickly customer issues are resolved. If you work in a retail environment, you may have expectations related to how customers are greeted when they walk through the door. Your list of personal expectations serves to supplement the formal tools provided by your organization.

Here are some expectation starters to help you develop your own list:

- If you are unable to complete your assigned caseload within the expected timeframe: _____

- If a client calls with a complaint: _____

- If you are unable to resolve a customer concern:_____

- If you can't finish your work by the end of the day/shift/agreed upon schedule: _____

- If you are going to arrive late: _____

- When traveling for business: _____

- If you are sick and cannot come to work: _____

- When you are participating in a team meeting: _____

- Return phone messages by: _____

- If you find yourself in a conflict with a teammate: _____

- Answer e-mails by: _____

- Greet walk-in customers by: _____

- Personal phone calls should be taken: _____

- Company computers and office equipment are to be used for personal purposes when: _____
- Our dress code is: _____
- To use your vacation time: _____

Here are a few more examples of performance expectations, written by managers who have attended *Painless Performance Conversations* workshops:

- Stay busy: When you are not serving customers, update the files, order supplies, and maintain your desk manual.
- Respond to customer inquiries within 1 hour.
- When your work is completed for the day, seek to help a coworker complete his or her work.
- Respond to voicemails and e-mails hourly.
- Prioritize work so that deadlines are met or let me know if there will be a problem meeting a deadline.
- If a personal call is received, it should be taken in the back and not at the front counter.
- If you are going to be late to work, call me on my cell phone as soon as you know you will be late so that we can plan for coverage.
- If you are sick with a fever, stay home.
- If the store is littered with paper or things are out of order, pick it up and straighten it out.

The list of expectations you create will be unique to you, your organization, and the work you are managing.

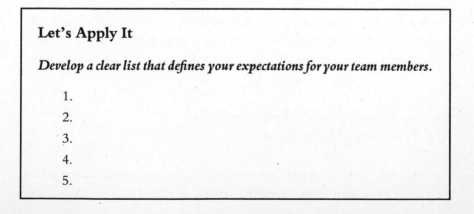

Let's Apply It

Develop a clear list that defines your expectations for your team members.

1.

2.

3.

4.

5.

Painless Perspective

Writing out your performance expectations helps clarify them in your own mind so that you can make them clear for employees.

Collaborating with Employees on Your List

Regardless of whether you are the regular manager or in a temporary assignment, a new manager or a seasoned veteran, a productive activity is to have a staff meeting to clarify your performance expectations and to hear from employees about their needs and expectations. The meeting should be a two-way conversation with employees, with the goal of hearing each other's perspectives. Essentially, the meeting will have two agenda items:

1. What does the staff expect from you to be effective on the job?
2. What do you expect from the staff that will allow them to be effective on the job? This is where you share your list of expectations.

The conversation itself will relieve some of the frustration that mounts while everyone is trying to figure out what it takes to be successful. Topics might include frequency of checking in/feedback, method of checking in (face to face, phone, e-mail), expectations for timeliness, customer service expectations (how fast should we respond), and so on. The details will depend on the workplace and the type of work you are doing.

Too often, managers hit the ground running and don't take the time to think about the success factors for each assignment. Remember that it takes time to clarify your expectations and that expectation setting requires conversations, the most valuable conversations you will have as a manager.

Setting Expectations When You Are in a Temporary Assignment

At times, you may be asked to take on the role of manager for a temporary amount of time with a new group of employees. These are sometimes called interim assignments. From an employee's perspective, it's kind of like having a substitute teacher. It's not unusual for employees to test the limits and see how far they can push the rules.

This scenario requires the same commitment to clarifying your expectations as when you are the regular manager. Although the circumstances may be different, your success and the employees' success still hinges on the clarity of your expectations. This means you have to be very clear and confident about what you stand for in terms of your values and expectations. Even if you are the manager for a short, six-week detail, it's imperative to kick off the engagement with a face-to-face conversation with employees about what working with you will be like.

When Expectations Change

Once team performance expectations are established, from the organization's perspective and from your personal perspective, brace yourself for change. It's inevitable: expectations *will* change over time. New priorities, new information, new leaders, new economic conditions, new competitive influences . . . these and many more factors can render your expectations and each employee's goals irrelevant by the time you evaluate the employee's progress. Because of this, you and the employee will need to acknowledge these shifts and adapt accordingly. Regardless, a clear performance plan helps each employee have direction and purpose in his or her work. When employees know what they are expected to produce, they can be independent and successful and thus can more easily adapt to change.

If you and the employee are not revisiting performance plans and expectations regularly, the employee may be left wondering, "What am I supposed to do now?" This is when performance stagnates and employees begin to feel as if their work is not valued. Without a process for evolving and updating expectations as the environment shifts, employees will be left feeling frustrated. Follow these steps to make sure your performance expectations reflect changes in the environment:

- Informally meet with each employee monthly. The purpose of this meeting is to revisit the employee's goals and your expectations and to make necessary revisions, based on changes in the environment.

- Document the changes you and the employee agree on. If you agree to change a deadline or cancel a project, make a note of it either in a performance log or in an e-mail to the employee that confirms and reinforces your agreement. Be sure to keep records of these discussions, as these notes can assist you when it's time to do the annual performance evaluation.

- Share new expectations as they arise. The organization will change direction. You may have new outcomes or results you would like to add to the employee's plan. As soon as you are aware of a change, have a quick discussion with the employee to share new information or have a team meeting to inform everyone of the change. Follow up with an e-mail to further document the changed expectations.

Sharing clear expectations with employees is the foundation of effective performance management. Organizational priorities change, new information is discovered, and budgets shift, all of which lead to adjustments in what we expect from employees. Maintaining a dialogue about expectations is imperative in today's rapidly changing work environment.

Reflection Question

What expectations have recently changed that you need to convey to your employees?

Conversation Checkpoints

- Employees can't read your mind. It's important to be clear with them about your expectations.
- Some expectations are defined by your organization through policies and practices.
- Every manager should have a list of his or her personal expectations, and the list should be shared with employees.
- Even if you are on a temporary assignment as the manager, it is important to establish your expectations.
- Expectations shift over time and require you to revisit and revise them.

From the Field

From James, Planning Manager:

As part of a Painless Performance Conversations workshop, planning manager James developed this list of clear basic expectations for his work group:

- **Arrive on time**. We work 8:00 AM to 5:00 PM, and we need your full contribution each day. Be here in time to start work at 8:00 AM. If you are going to be more than 10 minutes late, call the office and let me know.

- **Stay focused on work.** Leave web surfing, Internet videos, and newspaper reading for lunchtime or before or after work hours. Keep personal phone calls short and limit the number to two to three per day, unless there is an emergency.

- **Be prepared.** If you have meetings with customers or fellow staff members, be prepared. Know your materials/projects. Remember, you represent our organization. Collect relevant information from other participating staff members ahead of time to help you understand their perspectives.

- **Dress appropriately.** Casual does not mean sloppy, and blue jeans should be reserved for Fridays. If you are working with a customer in person, wear business attire.

- **Be a supportive team member.** We are in this together. Ask for help when you need it and offer help when you see another team member in need. Never dispute another team member's position in front of a customer. Discuss it with the person in private and seek a resolution if a conflict exists.

- **Take pride in your work.** Be thorough, accurate, and complete. What you write strongly influences how others perceive you. Spell check your work. Do the same with e-mails. Ask someone to proofread your work for you.

- **Be available during work hours.** Your contribution is important. Avoid absences when you are tasked to cover a particular function, such as the front desk. Arrange for someone to cover for you if your absence is unavoidable. Let someone know that you are leaving and when you expect to return.

- **Take breaks when you need them.** We all need to take a break throughout the day. However, keep them short and take them outside of the work area. Avoid standing around others' work areas, as it can be disruptive to them. Especially avoid taking breaks in the customer service areas.

- **Be polite.** Be courteous with customers and your coworkers. Resolve disagreements in private, away from customers. Talk to your manager if you can't resolve conflicts with your coworkers directly. Remember, we are all working for the same cause.

Sound Bites from the Field

James meets with new employees on their very first day of employment. He begins each conversation like this:

Welcome to our work group. We are very excited to have you on the team, and as your manager, I feel strongly that my job is to help you be wildly successful here. To be successful, I've developed a basic list of expectations. These are likely expectations that you share, and I'd like to take a moment to review them before we get into the nitty-gritty of our work.

After James reviews the list, he gives a copy to the employee and continues with the rest of the topics on the new hire orientation list.

Lessons Learned from the Field

James did a great job of identifying what success looks like for his staff. He expressed his expectations in brief, concise statements and then followed up with a deeper explanation. Some may say his expectations are common sense and too basic to put in writing. However, James found that once these fundamental expectations were written down, he rarely had to address these issues. Making these expectations clear freed him to focus on more critical, strategic initiatives.

The organization for which James works also has expectations, which are conveyed in policies, job descriptions, mission statements, and a strategic plan. However, few of these documents define the issues that James has outlined here. Developing this list allows James to be clear about the little things that may be taken for granted.

James meets with new employees on their first day of work and shares this list with them. He also reminds his long-term staff of these expectations at least quarterly during their regular staff meeting. His expectations are the foundation for how he manages his group. Again, they are not a replacement for job descriptions or policies; they are a supplement. They express James's core beliefs about what good performance looks like. Because James has set the groundwork for performance in his work unit, he rarely has to address these issues with staff in the course of their work.

Next Up

In Chapter 4 you'll see when and how to most effectively convey your performance expectations for employees. You will also apply a simple conversation model that will guide you through expectation-setting conversations.

4 | Share Your Expectations

Conveying a Picture of Success

High achievement always takes place in the framework of high expectations.
—Charles F. Kettering

As clear as your expectations may be in your head or on paper, they can be hard to clearly convey to employees. Instead of using clear language to express expectations, managers say things like:

- I'd like you to **take care** of that customer complaint today.
- Could you **prepare** that report for me?
- We need to make sure the office is **organized** before we go home tonight.

None of these statements clearly defines success for the employee, nor do they allow the employee to engage in a conversation to better understand your expectations. Each indicates that you expect something, but leave room for interpretation.

To convey the same expectations more specifically, you might say:

- Return that customer's call today and provide her with a response that is satisfactory to her and to our organization.
- By 5:00 PM today, compile and create a report on the number of daily inquiries.
- Before the end of our workday, please pick up the trash, straighten the magazines, and replenish the brochure supply in the waiting room.

When you discuss performance expectations with an employee, the conversation has the potential to be one-sided. It's easy to tell employees what you expect of them. You talk, and they listen. However, telling the employee what you expect does not always lead to a clear understanding of your message.

Painless Perspective

Defining expectations clearly and engaging employees in a conversation about them will help employees achieve success.

In Chapter 3 you learned where expectations come from (organizational expectations and your personal expectations). In this chapter you'll learn to share those expectations with employees in a way that involves them in the conversation and clarifies the success criteria. If you can master expectation-setting conversations, other performance conversations will be easy . . . even painless.

Opportunities to Talk about Expectations

You have the opportunity to lead expectation-setting conversations with employees at numerous times throughout the year. For example, expectation-setting conversations occur:

- When the employee is new to the organization
- When the employee has been transferred to your work group
- When you inherit a new work group
- At the start of a new year or new performance evaluation cycle
- At performance evaluation time
- When organizational/divisional/departmental goals change
- When a merger or acquisition has taken place
- When a reorganization has taken place
- After a layoff has taken place
- Informally in casual conversations throughout the year

In fact, as manager of your work group, you are setting expectations in every conversation you have with employees. What you spend your time talking about will send a message to employees about what is important. Therefore, you must capitalize on these opportunities to reinforce your expectations. You'll have expectation-setting opportunities during:

- Hiring interviews
- New employee orientation
- Regular staff meetings
- One-on-one meetings with employees
- Hallway conversations
- Site visits
- Break room conversations
- Lunch outings
- Drives to a work site

You have opportunities throughout every day to share and clarify expectations with employees. The key is to recognize the opportunities and seize them.

As you are seizing the opportunity to engage employees in a conversation about expectations, remember that your list of expectations must be simple and easy to remember. In that way, your expectations are not much different from a politician's stump speech. Every successful politician has a stump speech that defines what he or she stands for. The best stump speeches leave an imprint. Politicians repeat their message over and over at every opportunity so that voters know exactly what they represent. Managers also need a stump speech to ensure that employees know what they represent. Your stump speech should include your expectations for performance, emphasizing what is important to you and to the organization. The stump speech might focus on a key initiative, an overarching value, or a priority, such as workplace safety.

Painless Perspective

Think carefully about what you represent. Have a stump speech that clearly conveys what is important to you.

Tips for Making the Most of Expectation-Setting Opportunities

Here are a few tips to help you get ready for your expectation-setting opportunities:

- **Lay out a clear vision.** In the course of your formal and informal conversations with employees, use phrases such as, "This year, if our team accomplishes just three things, we'll be able to claim success. The three most important things for our team are ____, ____, and ____."

- **Describe your ideal.** During expectation-setting conversation opportunities, use phrases such as, "To be successful in this work unit, I expect you will ____." You can finish this sentence with qualitative measures, quantitative measures, or the specific behaviors you expect, such as, "I expect that you will complete 50 case files each day," or "I expect you will return customer phone calls within 3 hours of receipt."

- **Be specific about the end result.** When doling out assignments, it's easy to assume the employee sees the task the same way you do. The next time you ask an employee to complete a task or to take on a new project, don't forget to include this important sentence in your conversation:

  "This project will be successful if _____."

  By clearly defining how you see the end product, the employee is more likely to envision it as you do.

The Sound of an Informal Expectation-Setting Opportunity

You will have multiple opportunities to clarify your expectations every day. For example, if you are in a project meeting and the team is exploring options for solving a critical system problem, you may interject into the discussion that you believe the project will be successful if the customers are able to access their account data from their mobile devices. That is your vision and your expectation. As obvious as your point may be, restating the expectation will refocus the team on their ultimate goal.

In another example, assume you are driving to a remote worksite with one of your employees. Along the way the employee suggests changing the way supplies are delivered and logged. In the course of the conversation you might say, "Remember back at the last team meeting when I said our two major goals this year are to reduce costs and to improve our customer service rating by 10 percent? This idea you have for streamlining the delivery and tracking of supplies may be aligned to that goal. How do you think changing our supply process will contribute to the achievement of those goals?" By encouraging the employee to explore how his idea supports the work group's goals, you are reinforcing the expectations while encouraging the employee to consider how he contributes to the work unit.

Expectation-setting opportunities will spring up when you least expect them. So, it's important to be clear about what's important.

Reflection Questions

What expectations do you need to share that you haven't yet expressed or haven't clearly expressed? What opportunities do you have to clarify your expectations?

Leading a Formal Conversation about Performance Expectations

Although expectation-setting opportunities throughout the course of a regular workday are common, you will also want to initiate or schedule specific conversations that allow you to lay out your expectations. These more formal, one-on-one meetings may occur with new employees, when you or they are new to the work group, or when you find that an employee has lost focus on the priorities you have established. To be successful in these manager-initiated conversations, you'll again want to be prepared.

Follow this agenda when leading an expectation-setting conversation with a new employee or with an employee whom you intend to redirect.

1. **State the purpose of the conversation.**
   The purpose of the conversation may be:
   □ To establish clear expectations for performance.
   □ To define what success looks like.
   □ To ensure the employee can thrive in his or her role.

2. **Review critical organizational expectations.**
   □ Share copies of the organization's mission, vision, and/or values.
   □ Explain how your work group supports these organizational expectations.
   □ Show the employee how his or her work supports the organization's goals.
   □ Remind the employee how his or her contribution, on a daily basis, matters.

3. **Review your list of expectations.**
   □ Share a written copy of your list with the employee. Give the employee a copy of your list to keep.
   □ Review each item on the list in detail.
   □ Ask the employee if he or she has questions about the list or if there is anything he or she would like to add.
   □ Make necessary changes to your list of expectations based on the employee's feedback.

4. **Ask the employee what he or she needs.** Engage the employee in a dialogue about the expectations you have set forth. Ask questions such as:
   □ What do you need to meet the organizational expectations?
   □ What expectation will be the most challenging for you?

□ What do you need to meet the expectations on the list?

□ What concerns do you have about the definition of success that has been shared with you?

□ How can I help you meet these expectations?

□ What obstacles do you anticipate?

□ What expectations do you have for this job?

□ What expectations do you have of me, your manager?

5. **Express confidence.**

□ Tell the employee that your goal is to help him or her be successful.

□ Encourage the employee to come to you with questions or concerns.

□ Express your confidence in the employee's ability to be successful.

The Sound of a Formal Expectation-Setting Conversation

If you haven't experienced a productive expectation-setting conversation in your career, the preceding outline may sound strange. But having a productive conversation is actually very simple. The most basic expectation-setting conversation you initiate will be with new employees. Here's an example of how this conversation might sound between a manager and a new employee named Brynn.

1. **State the purpose of the conversation.**

Manager: Hi, Brynn. I'm really looking forward to having you on the team. My goal as your manager is to help you be successful here. I'd like to spend a little time defining success so that we are on the same page. If we are both clear about the expectations for success, we'll be much more focused on getting there. Okay?

Brynn: Sounds good to me.

2. **Review critical organizational expectations.**

Manager: Let's start with what you already know, and we'll build from there. What do you know about our organization's mission and vision?

Brynn: Well, I know that the mission statement is hanging in the hallways and that the vision is to serve the community's needs. I know we are supposed to be responsible with our dollars. We don't want to waste the organization's resources.

Manager: Good. Anything else?

Brynn: I know that my job is to process payments so that we can accurately account for the money that comes in and out of the organization. I know that I'm part of a team that is ultimately responsible for producing financial statements. I know that we've just implemented a new system to help monitor the financials, so I know leveraging technology is part of the vision for how we do business.

Manager: That's a great start! The mission statement you see in the hallways guides what we do every day and reminds us to stay focused on the service we are providing to our customers. That's why we exist. In fact, there's also a copy of the mission and vision posted in your cubicle. We keep that front and center to remind us why we're here.

Brynn: Thanks.

3. **Review your list of expectations.**

Manager's List of Expectations for Brynn

Success in this work unit means you are expected to:

- Arrive to every commitment on time or early. Late is late.

- Be prepared by bringing all the necessary tools, information, and equipment to each meeting.

- Respond to customers promptly by returning phone calls within 24 hours and acknowledging walk-in customers within 15 seconds of their arrival.

- Support your teammates by lending a hand and by covering for them when they need help. They will do the same for you.

- Be accountable by keeping your voicemail message up to date and calling me at least an hour before your shift if you are going to be late or absent.

Manager: I'd also like to share with you a list of my expectations for success in this work unit. This list reflects my priorities for how we do business in this department. It's important for you to understand these expectations right up front so that you will know how we define *success*. No one wants surprises along the way. Let's look at the list item by item.

Brynn: Okay.

Manager: The first thing on the list is "Arrive to every meeting on time or early." I'm a real stickler for promptness. I believe that if we agree on a time to begin, either a meeting or the start of the day, we should meet that commitment. To me, 5 minutes late is late. I also expect that you will always bring the necessary information and tools to each meeting (paper, pen, agenda, working documents). I guess it's my scouting experience, but I believe we should be prepared at all times. How do you feel about that?

Brynn: I can understand that. We don't want to waste time waiting for people.

Manager: Exactly! The next expectation on the list is that you will always leave a current voicemail message on your phone. Customer service is really important in this work unit. In fact, we pride ourselves on being responsive and customer-focused. So, if you are going to be out of the office for any more than a few hours, update your voicemail message so that callers will know when they can expect to hear back from you. Also, we return every phone call within 24 hours of receipt and acknowledge each walk-in customer within 15 seconds. These are all standards of service that our team has developed collaboratively and agreed upon. What questions do you have, Brynn?

Brynn: What if I can't return a call within 24 hours? What if I'm out sick or on vacation?

Manager: That's a great question. If you know you aren't going to be able to meet one of our service standards, you are expected to let either me or a coworker know so that we can take care of it. We all cover for each other. Just as your coworkers will help you stay up to date with your work, you are expected to do the same for them. Teamwork is really important around here. What other questions do you have?

Brynn: That makes sense. I think I understand. What else is on the list?

Manager: The last two items on the list relate to teamwork and accountability. As we just discussed, everyone here is expected to support one another. If you see a coworker who needs help, lend a hand. If you are asked to fill in for a teammate when he or she is out of the office, you're expected to do it as part of your job. We depend on one another, so it's important that we consistently help each other be successful. The last item on the list is about what to do when you are going to be late or absent. If you are running late for work, please call me directly on my cell phone as soon as possible, preferably an hour before your shift begins. I also expect you will request vacation days as far in advance as possible and avoid leaving us without coverage at all costs. I believe that every employee must take responsibility for his or her results. If you make a mistake, and we all do, just admit it and work to fix it. Again, my goal is to help you be successful, and I need to know what's happening with you to make that happen.

Brynn: What if an emergency comes up, and I can't call you an hour before my shift begins?

Manager: I understand that things happen. We can't always predict the future. However, I believe you can minimize the impact of those emergencies by being attentive to how your actions affect the workplace.

Brynn: Okay. That sounds logical to me.

4. **Ask the employee what he or she needs.**

Manager: So, Brynn, that's my list of expectations. I know it might be a little overwhelming at this point, but I'd like you to think about a few things. First, what do you need to be able to meet the expectations we've just discussed?

Brynn: Oh, wow. That's a tough question. I guess I just need to know that I can come to you if I have questions. I also hope you'll let me know if I'm not meeting your expectations.

Manager: Absolutely! We are in this together. Please come to me if you have a question about anything. I'm here to help. As you think about those expectations, are there any that you think may be especially challenging for you?

Brynn: Not really. I'm pretty conscientious and prompt. I like to get my work done on time or early. As I think about it, these expectations aren't really difficult to achieve. Still it's good to know where you are coming from.

Manager: Good. What do you expect of me as your manager?

Brynn: Wow, that's a good question. I guess I expect you'll tell me how I'm doing and let me know if there's something that's not right. I also expect that I'll be treated fairly.

Manager: Those are fair expectations and ones I'm committed to. What else?

Brynn: Well, I have questions about the work processes and deadlines, but I think we'll be going over all of that in our meeting with Jane later today, right?

5. **Express confidence.**

Manager: Right. We'll get into the details of your duties in a little while. For now, I wanted to lay out the expectations for success and let you know that my goal is to help you be successful here. Please let me know what you need along the way.

Brynn: Okay. I'll do that.

Manager: In the meantime, I'm confident that you are going to have a great career here. Welcome to the group.

During the conversation, the manager gave this list of expectations to Brynn.

Being prepared with this list of expectations allowed the manager to be successful in this conversation and engage Brynn in a two-way conversation about the expectations. There was room for Brynn to contribute, and the manager created an environment where Brynn felt supported.

Let's Apply It

Think about the expectation-setting conversations you have with new employees. Apply the five steps in the expectation-setting conversation agenda learned earlier in this chapter.

1. How will you open the conversation?

2. What organizational expectations do you need to discuss?

3. Is your written list of expectations clear, prepared, and ready to share?

4. Do you have specific examples that make your point?

5. How will you ask the employee what he or she needs to be able to meet your expectations?

6. How will you conclude the conversation and sincerely express your confidence in the employee?

7. On a scale of 1 to 10, how comfortable are you in having this conversation? Why?

8. What do you expect the outcome of this conversation will be?

9. What will happen if you do not have this conversation?

10. How will you ensure this is a two-way conversation that engages the employee?

If you align expectations with reality, you will never be disappointed.

—Terrell Owens

Keeping the Conversation Going

In expectation-setting conversations, it's easy to do all the talking. And, even if you attempt to engage the employee with an open-ended question, you may be met with a brief or nonexistent response. Even Brynn, in our example, had very little to say. Great managers use conversation starters to keep the discussion moving forward, to engage the employee in a dialogue, and to avoid surprises down the road. When an employee nods "yes," you really don't know if he or she sees the expectation as you do or if he or she is simply agreeing with you to avoid conflict. Although a head nod is a common response, it doesn't always mean the employee gets it. Your goal should be to encourage employees to ask questions and be engaged. Follow your statement of expectations with these prompts:

- What might this look like in the course of your day?
- Which of these expectations might be more challenging for you to meet?
- What is likely to get in your way?
- How do you feel about these expectations?
- What expectations would you like to add to the list?
- What do you need from me to be able to meet these expectations?

With practice you'll be able to lead expectation-setting conversations with confidence.

Conversation Checkpoints

- Expectations should be discussed routinely throughout the employee's employment.
- Performance expectations should be discussed informally and formally in the workplace.

- As a manager, have a stump speech that regularly conveys your expectations for success in the workplace.

- Reinforce your expectations as much as possible. They represent you and what you stand for.

- The formal expectation-setting conversation follows five steps that include a dialogue with the employee about his or her perspectives.

- Keeping the conversation going with thought-provoking questions is as important as initiating the conversation in the first place.

From the Field

From Elaine, Library Manager:

My staff is well trained and highly qualified to serve the community. I take for granted that a trained library professional knows what good customer service looks like. To me, that means the facility is kept neat and clean. It means that when customers approach the service desk they are greeted warmly and that our services are innovative. It means we create an experience that makes customers return again and again.

I've just inherited a new branch library and am surprised to find that the staff is less than attentive to our customers. For example, last week during a brief tour of the facility, I found trash throughout the building, an unattended service desk with customers waiting, and books stacked up in the returns bin waiting to be reshelved. As a result, our circulation numbers have been declining and our customer visits have also dropped.

I've told the staff I value customer service and innovation, but they don't seem to be picking up on my priorities. I don't want to beat them over the head with it, but the current situation is not acceptable. Several staff members have shared with me that they are not satisfied with the direction the library has been going, but they don't know how to make the necessary changes. They are looking to me to lead the charge.

My plan is to develop a clear list of expectations that apply to all library employees which will create a baseline for expected performance. My list will include expectations like:

- If you see trash around the facility and you are not with a customer, stop and pick it up.

- When there are books in the return bin, check them back in and put them on the cart to be reshelved.

- If you have more than three customers in line, call a coworker or a supervisor and ask for assistance.

I'm going to share the list with the staff at the next staff meeting and let them know that these three items are just the start. I'll ask them to work in small groups to brainstorm other expectations that illustrate what success looks like in our organization. I'll encourage them to think about what it takes to create a well-respected, credible library in terms of the staff's contribution. Together we'll explore their lists, combine ideas, and agree on a list that everyone can support. I can then use that list to orient new employees who join our team. I hope that we can create "our list" so that they will buy into the need to improve service levels.

However, I'm worried that this will sound like I'm forcing my ideas onto the team. How can I share my expectations with this seasoned staff without creating resentment or impacting morale?

Sound Bites from the Field

Elaine's plan to involve the staff in creating common expectations is a good one. She may want to begin the meeting this way:

> I know that this team is one of the most highly qualified and seasoned teams within the library system, and I respect your ideas and experience. Right now our circulation is declining, and our customer visits are down. That troubles me, and a number of you have shared with me that you are worried about it, too. I expect that we are going to work together to make this branch library a place the community values. To build that kind of reputation, we all need to be clear about our expectations of one another. I'd like to hear your expectations for how the branch could/should operate, and along the way, I'll share some of my ideas too.

Lessons Learned from the Field

Elaine has stepped into a challenging environment that will take some time to change. Because she is clear about her vision, she can confidently start a conversation with employees about performance expectations. By enlisting employees in the conversation about what success looks like, employees will be more likely to support the final list of expectations. They may even begin to help one another live up to the agreements they've made.

Elaine's approach allows her to express her expectations and reinforce her stump speech about customer service while engaging her staff in a thoughtful dialogue about success.

Next Up

There are four critical mind-sets that allow you to lead a performance conversation painlessly, in a way the employee will be able to hear and understand. The four mind-sets of a painless performance conversation are:

- Lead with behavior.
- Eliminate judgment.
- Inquire with purpose.
- Be clear.

In Chapter 5 you'll begin to explore the first of the four mind-sets. The first mind-set, lead with behavior, allows you to identify specific steps an employee can take to improve performance.

5 | Lead with Behavior

Separating Actions from Attitudes

Behavior is a mirror in which everyone displays his own image.
—Johann Wolfgang von Goethe

Have you ever worked with an employee who had a bad attitude?

Have you ever tried to change an employee with an attitude problem?

When you have attempted to change an employee's attitude, were you successful?

A conversation that focuses on an employee's attitude can, and likely will, spiral out of control because you and the employee will be talking about something that is not observable. Because attitudes are deeply embedded in the employee's belief system and changing the employee's beliefs can be a challenging task, performance conversations must focus on observable behaviors. Rather than beginning performance conversations focused on attitude, lead with behavior.

Starting the conversation by focusing on an employee's attitude will backfire for two reasons. First, describing the employee's attitude does not help him or her understand what's being done that is unacceptable. For example, if you say, "John, you need to focus more so that you can improve your performance," John will likely say that he *is* focused. At that point the conflict is about whether or not he is focused. Instead, if you describe the behaviors you have observed, he is more likely to engage in the conversation. For example, you might say, "John, I've noticed that your tracking forms were not completed for our last three one-on-one meetings."

Second, focusing on the employee's attitude does not leave room in the conversation to guide the employee to a productive change. If you lead the conversation with a statement about John's lack of focus, the conversation is more general in nature, and he won't really know what to do differently. If you can give John a specific example about what he did or didn't do that had an impact on the job, there is room in the conversation to explore options. A more specific example might sound like, "John, during our last three meetings when you did not bring your completed tracking forms, we were unable to review the progress you've made." By leading with the specific behavior you have observed, John is less likely to be immediately defensive and more likely to understand what he needs to do differently in the future.

Behavior versus Attitude

Attitudes are the subconscious transfer of feelings to the workplace. Attitudes define who people are, which means they are very personal. They are internal, are intangible, and cannot be seen; they are rooted in emotions and beliefs. Although it is impossible to see attitudes, they can be perceived and felt when they are projected in behaviors. For example, you may perceive that an employee has a negative attitude toward customers. Yet, you don't know what is going on inside the employee's head. You have come to your conclusion by observing the employee's behaviors. If the employee interrupts customers before they are finished talking and the employee doesn't smile when serving customers, you may believe the employee has a bad attitude. It's the behavior that allows you to draw a conclusion about the employee's attitude.

Behaviors, on the other hand, are what people do or do not do. They are observable, actionable, and tangible. Behaviors are external and can be seen and quantified. They produce an outcome. Behaviors can represent the employee's attitude, but this is not always the case. For example, if you observe that an employee begins working on files and paperwork every time a customer enters the store, leaving coworkers to serve the customer, you might believe the employee has a bad attitude and doesn't care about customer service. The facts, however, are just that the employee is working on files instead of serving customers. The attitude that affected the behavior is unclear.

Your beliefs don't make you a better person. Your behavior does.

—Unknown

Naming Attitudes and Behaviors

Before you initiate a potentially painful conversation with an employee about a performance issue, take a moment to clarify the behavior you have observed that is leading you to have the conversation. If you begin the conversation with your perception of the employee's attitude, he or she is likely to resist your conversational efforts. Instead, lead with the behavior you have observed. Table 5.1 includes some potentially painful conversation examples presented first with a focus on attitude and then with a focus on behavior.

Table 5.1 Leading with Attitude versus Leading with Behavior

Attitude Manager leads with, *"Lately it seems like you've been _____."*	Behavior Manager leads with, *"I noticed that you _____."*
Selfish	Requested to take the afternoon off before meeting all customer requests for the day
Inflexible	Faced a difficult decision with the Drake file and decided to deny the request rather than searching for a creative solution that will meet the customer's needs as well as the organization's needs
Lacking motivation or commitment	Have not signed up for the certification class that's required for promotion
A good team player	Offered to help coworkers when they were in need of assistance with the INT project
Lazy	Arrived to work 10 minutes after the agreed-upon time
Not customer-focused	Left for lunch before returning a call to a customer when the customer was expecting your call
Careless	Missed three production deadlines this week
Self-promoting	Argued about why you should have been promoted instead of someone else
Acting like a know-it-all	Interrupted your colleagues during the staff meeting to make your point
Stubborn	Were unwilling to make a change when the majority of the group believed it was the right thing to do
Resistant to change	Did not use the new process that the team has adopted

Painless Perspective

It's easier to ask an employee to **do** something differently than it is to ask him or her to **be** someone different.

When you focus the conversation on the employee's attitude, you will likely get a defensive reaction. The reaction is the natural fight-or-flight response. If the employee feels attacked, whether it is emotionally, personally, or physically, the reaction is to withdraw or fight back. When feeling under attack, the employee will stop listening and become more concerned about his or her next response rather than a solution.

Raising the issue of an employee's attitude may increase that employee's awareness that a problem exists. However, the employee may not agree with how you have defined his or her attitude, as it is an intangible observation, and may be more inclined to offer a defense than to listen to what you have to say. You might say that an employee's attitude is lazy or unenthusiastic, but really, the employee is feeling tired and burned out. You might label the employee's attitude as defiant, yet the employee may actually be feeling scared. Remember, your goal as a manager is to help the employee change the behavior, and you can change behavior only if you minimize the defensiveness in the conversation by focusing on what the person is doing rather than who the person is or what you think of him or her. Once you have had an impact on the employee's behavior, a change in attitude might follow. Although your ultimate goal may be to affect the employee's attitude, start with behavior.

Performance conversations can be delicate. If you focus on the person and his or her attitude, you are referencing that person's character, value, and worth as a human being; in short, your focus on attitude quickly becomes personal. When you focus on observable behaviors, you identify specific factual evidence that is affecting the workplace, and in the process, you take the individual's character out of the conversation.

By factually stating the situation and focusing on what the person did or didn't do, rather than on who the person is, it will be easier for you and the employee to have a nondefensive conversation. Table 5.2 illustrates what it sounds like to focus on the employee's attitude versus the employee's behavior.

Table 5.2 Focusing on Attitude versus Focusing on Behavior

Focus on Attitude	Focus on Behavior
"You have such a negative outlook that your coworkers don't want to work with you anymore."	"When you don't greet your coworkers in the morning, they perceive that as disinterest. This makes them less willing to work with you."
"Lately, you are not giving enough priority to your status reports, which makes me think you don't care."	"Three times this month the status report deadlines were not met."
"You seem to be distracted and more careless with your work recently."	"Your reports have included 10 percent more errors this month than in the past three months."
"You know, Zachary, you come across as a know-it-all in meetings, and your teammates resent your contributions."	"You interrupted your teammates at least five times during the meeting. When you do this, they feel as if you do not value their work."

In each example, virtually the same message is being delivered. In the left column, where the focus is on attitude, the employee is more likely to respond defensively. The employee is less likely to respond defensively to the statements in the right column because they are statements of behavior. In performance conversations, there is a greater opportunity for you to explore the root cause of the behavior and help the employee improve, rather than trying to define the employee's attitude.

Evidence of Behavior

Behaviors are evidence that can be solidly presented in conversations about performance. The behaviors that concern you about an employee's work may fall into a variety of categories, including:

- Spoken words: What the employee *says* is behavioral evidence.

- Actions: What the employee *does* is behavioral evidence.

- Reactions: How the employee *responds* in specific situations is behavioral evidence.

- Data or output: The products that *result or don't result* from the employee's efforts are behavioral evidence.

- Physical space: The *environment* the employee creates is behavioral evidence.

The more tangible the evidence you can describe to the employee, the more clearly he or she will be able to see your concern about the performance.

Painless Perspective

Define the behavioral evidence you have observed when discussing a performance issue with an employee.

What You Observe versus What You Assume

Another way to distinguish between behaviors and attitudes is to be aware of what you observe and the conclusions that result from what you have seen. We all make assumptions. Have you ever labeled an employee (for example, as unmotivated, smart, self-interested) and later found evidence to prove your assumptions wrong? Regardless, when yourassumptions cloud the facts, performance conversations become painful.

When a situation catches your attention, two things happen in your brain, as illustrated in Figure 5.1. First, you notice what is going on, and second, you make assumptions about what you've seen. It's an automatic response. You notice an employee's appearance, the words that person chooses, and the behaviors he or she displays. You notice the reactions of others to the employee's behavior. You notice the results of that employee's contribution. You notice facts.

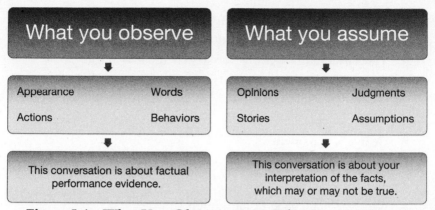

Figure 5.1   What You Observe versus What You Assume

At the same time, your imagination creates a story about what you are noticing. Your thoughts, conclusions, and beliefs about the employee are being developed at the same time you are noticing the behaviors. Assumptions are the result of your brain processing what you have observed, and your assumptions may or may not be accurate. The trick is to filter your assumptions before they cloud your conclusions.

When you let your assumptions dominate your conversations with employees, you often end up telling yourself a story that may or may not be true. For example, it is easy to assume that an employee is not committed to the organization if she takes every Monday and Friday off. It's easy to assume the employee is taking advantage of her paid leave to extend her weekends. In reality, it is possible that the employee is caring for a sick relative whose doctors are available only on Mondays and Fridays. Making assumptions, without all of the facts, leads you to draw conclusions, create stories about the person's background, judge his or her motives, and focus on what you think is true rather than what is really the truth.

Men occasionally stumble over the truth, but most of them pick themselves up and hurry off as if nothing ever happened.

—Winston Churchill

If you are thinking, "I don't do that. I am always objective when assessing work-related situations," consider these examples:

- You **observed** that George arrived late to work three times this week.
- You **observed** that George left work early twice this week.
- You **observed** that George has less energy than usual.

From these observations, it's easy to jump to a variety of assumptions and conclusions, for example:

- George is unmotivated.
- George is lazy.
- George has a bad attitude.
- George is not a good fit for this job.
- George is not a good employee.
- George is having personal problems.

The truth may be very different from what you assume. In a conversation with George that focuses on what you've observed, you may learn that George is struggling to keep up with work and school or that he has a sick child at home. You may learn that George is working two jobs in order to pay his bills. You may also learn that George is applying for new jobs because he is no longer engaged by the work you have to offer. Based on what you learn from George, your conclusions may shift.

Painless Perspective

Although a bad attitude may legitimately affect the employee's performance, it is best to focus on and document the observable behaviors that indicate the attitude rather than the attitude itself.

If the conversation focuses on what you assume—that George is unmotivated, is lazy, and has a bad attitude—it's likely that George will become defensive and shut down before you ever uncover the truth. Focusing on what you assume leads to a painful conversation because defensiveness will get in the way of searching for an appropriate solution.

Leading with assumptions and conclusions, before hearing George out, ensures that he will be less willing to participate in the conversation. The ultimate goal is to help George improve his performance. To do so, he will need to be involved in determining the solution.

> ## Reflection Question
>
> *What do you focus on most when assessing employee performance: what you observe, or what you assume?*

Here are other examples of how easy it is to jump to conclusions from the behaviors you observe:

- You **observe** that the employee arrived late to work today and has done so at least two times for the past three weeks.
- You **assume** that the employee really doesn't care about the work or the organization.

*   *   *

- You **observe** an employee talking with a major customer on the telephone, and the employee is arguing with the customer, using a raised voice.
- You **assume** the employee has created the problem with the customer.

*   *   *

- You **observe** that one of your team members was playing games on her phone during today's team meeting.
- You **assume** that she is not a very good team player and that she doesn't care about the team.

In each example, what you noticed was factual, verifiable, and indisputable. Everything observed was a behavior. Each assumption, however, was a conclusion that stemmed from the behavior, and the assumption may or may not be the truth. Without a conversation to explore the facts of the situation, it's easy to label the behavior you have observed and be wrong.

Painless Perspective

The behaviors you observe are more reliable than the assumptions you make.

When beginning a conversation with an employee where you intend to deliver feedback about performance, remember to stick with the behaviors you have observed, rather than what you assume to be true. The more you realize that your assumptions may be wrong, the more effective you will be at using conversations to drive the performance you expect.

Let's Apply It

Answer the following questions, considering a performance-related conversation you've recently had with an employee.

1. With whom did you have the performance conversation?
2. What issue or issues were addressed?
3. What did you observe in this situation?
4. What did you assume about the situation?
5. What did you focus on more during the conversation: what you observed or what you assumed?
6. What was the outcome? Did you focus on the right things?

Focusing on Attitude Can Lead to Discrimination

In addition to being unproductive, focusing on the employee's attitude and making assumptions can be costly, not only for the organization, but for the manager personally. Describing an employee based on attitude, rather than behavior, can be viewed as discriminatory. For example, if I describe Franco as lazy but do not define the behavior that led me to that assumption, Franco could link my assumption to my beliefs about his national origin or race, not the behavior I observed.

Employment lawyers and courts often interpret the word *attitude* as a kind of discrimination, which may actually be based on age, race, gender, or disability. When the focus of your conversation with an employee is on his or her attitude and the assumptions you've made about that attitude, it is possible for the employee, and for the courts, to link your perspective to a protected class. For example, if Franco is of a certain national origin and it is found that the organization has a pattern of discriminating against employees of that national origin, your comments about Franco's laziness will become evidence that Franco was, in fact, discriminated against, even if that was not your intention. Although your comments would be just one piece of evidence in a larger case, they contribute to the body of evidence against the organization. As a result, both you and your employer can be held liable.

In another example, let's say you observe that an employee is pregnant and assume that she will not be as committed to the workplace once the baby arrives. Then, you make job assignments based on that assumption. Adjusting those assignments based solely on the fact that your employee is pregnant could be perceived as violating the Pregnancy Discrimination Act. The act stipulates that women who are pregnant or affected by pregnancy-related conditions must be treated in the same manner as other employees with similar abilities or limitations.

If you observe that an employee is older than age 40 and assume that he is not flexible or willing to learn about new technologies, you may be violating the Age Discrimination in Employment Act. Of course, to be held liable for such violations you would need to act upon your assumptions. Nevertheless, assumptions that are not explored and verified with behaviors can lead to poor and costly decisions.

Conversation Checkpoints

- Concentrating a conversation on an employee's bad attitude is not likely to lead to sustained performance improvement.
- Attitudes are the beliefs employees have. They are internal and intangible.
- Behaviors are what an employee does that is observable and tangible.
- Focus performance conversations on behaviors rather than attitudes to have a significant impact on the employee's willingness to converse.
- Talking about an employee's attitude could be misconstrued and lead to potential claims of discrimination.

From the Field

From David, School Administrator:

In addition to being responsible for a school of 1,000 children and 40 teachers, I oversee the operations of the school's front office. My expectation is that everyone on the campus is responsive and attentive to our students, their families, and other members of our community. Our goal is to create a welcoming environment for the entire neighborhood. That's why I was so frustrated with our front desk receptionist, Carole. Carole has served as the receptionist at our school for over 20 years, and she has seen it all. In fact, she often acts like she just doesn't care anymore. She is indifferent to parents who come into the office and acts like she doesn't care about their issues. Carole has been described by her coworkers as "cold" and "unfriendly." Today I received a complaint from a parent who said Carole was "a callous woman who shouldn't be working with children."

I know I have to talk with Carole about her attitude. She is the face of our school, and it is important that she projects a positive impression. Talking about her attitude is likely to backfire, though.

Sound Bites from the Field

David might open the conversation with Carole this way:

Carole, today I received a call from a parent who was not happy with an encounter she had with you. Mrs. Finley said she came in to get information about registration. She said that when she asked you for the information you didn't greet her warmly, and she said you told her she had to come back in two weeks. She said that you came across as callous and uncaring. What happened?

Carole may respond with defensiveness. She will also have her side of the story, which deserves to be heard. By relaying the behaviors that have been reported and leading the conversation with behaviors rather than describing Carole's attitude, David can get to the root of the issue. He now has an opportunity to focus the conversation on the interaction with the parent, rather than trying to defend his assumption that Carole has a bad attitude.

Lessons Learned from the Field

David is on target with his approach. Carole will not be able to explore alternatives if she is defending herself from an attack on her attitudes and beliefs. Carole has a perspective on the situation, and David will need to hear her out before he can shift the conversation to focusing on what Carole could have done differently.

Once David has considered Carole's side of the story, he will focus the conversation on a common goal to which he and Carole can agree. In this case, David and Carole both value responsiveness and friendliness. They agree that it is important to create an inviting, warm environment for the entire community. When David talks with Carole, he will remind her of this common expectation and describe specific instances and interactions where the customer felt unwelcomed. David will need to be as specific as possible, quoting Carole and the parent when possible. Only when Carole sees the impact of her behaviors on others will she be able to make lasting adjustments.

Next Up

In Chapter 6 you'll explore the second of the four painless performance conversation mind-sets: eliminate judgment. By comparing the facts with your expectations, you will be able to identify critical gaps in the employee's performance. Defining performance gaps allows you to communicate the need for change.

6 | Eliminate Judgment

Focusing on Performance Evidence

People seldom resist learning to change their attitude, behavior, or performance when the feedback is based on accurate assessments and observational data that validate the assessments.

—Robert Hargrove

Engaged employees are involved in and enthusiastic about their work. Gallup, Inc., in its Gallup Daily tracking series, found that when managers give little or no feedback to employees, 4 of 10 workers report being actively disengaged. Disengaged employees are not emotionally connected to their workplaces and are less likely to put in discretionary effort. When employees are disengaged they often produce shoddy work, have low morale, and reduce organizational output.

Performance conversations with disengaged employees are likely to be painful. Likewise, if you create an environment that engages employees, your performance conversations will more likely be painless. One way to create an engaging work environment is to give frequent, evidence-based feedback that is offered with the intent to help.

It's Up to You

Part of your job as a manager is to give feedback to your employees to help them meet and exceed your performance expectations. It should be easy, right? Just share your perspectives with employees, and they will improve, grow, and develop. As easy as this concept sounds, most managers struggle with giving feedback that is constructive, specific, illustrative, productive, and received the way it is intended.

One reason giving feedback is tough is because managers often don't give feedback; they make judgments. Performance conversations will be most impactful when you focus on judgment-free evidence and on the gap between what you expect and what you have observed. The second critical mind-set for a painless performance conversation is to eliminate judgment from your performance discussions.

Judgment versus Evidence

In the previous chapter you learned to distinguish between behaviors and attitudes and to begin performance conversations with behaviors. Behaviors are identified by concentrating on what you observe rather than making assumptions about what you have seen or heard. The next step is to center your attention on specific evidence you've noticed, rather than jumping to conclusions about what you have seen. Here's the difference:

Judgments include opinions or conclusions. Judgments are after-the-fact and based on your perception of the situation. When you make a judgment about an employee's behavior, you are making an assumption about what the person is doing and applying a general term to it. For example, you might describe an employee as having a strong work ethic. Or when you describe an employee's contribution to the team, you say the person is not a good team player. Our natural reactions are often emotion-driven and value-laden.

Evidence, on the other hand, is the process of providing judgment-free facts or data to support performance improvement. It is any statement based on information gathered informally or formally about something that can be seen, heard, measured, or counted. Evidence is not based on personal feelings and subjective opinions. It focuses on behaviors, actions, decisions, and choices.

Painless Perspective

Give more evidence-based feedback free of judgment.

Table 6.1 includes a few more distinctions between performance feedback based on judgment and feedback based on evidence.

Table 6.1   Judgment versus Evidence

Performance Feedback Based on Judgment	Performance Feedback Based on Evidence
Opinion	Factual
Conclusions	Proof
Conceptual	Concrete
Emotion-driven	Free of emotional influence
Provided for the benefit of the manager	Provided for the benefit of the employee
Intended to force change	Intended to influence growth

An essential principle of a painless performance conversation is to recognize this important difference. Here are a few examples:

Judgment—"You didn't prepare enough for that important presentation."

Evidence—"There were details and statistics that were not included in your presentation. For example. . . . "

*   *   *

Judgment—"You are not carrying your weight in the office."

Evidence—"You have completed three case files this week. Your peers are completing an average of six case files per week, and the standard is five files per week."

*   *   *

Judgment—"You did a great job today! Nice work!"

Evidence—"Your ideas for solving the Jones complaint were innovative and effective. You gave the customer several options, all of which were appropriate given the situation."

*   *   *

Judgment—"Many of your assignments are sloppy and unfinished."

Evidence—"This month there were four projects that were not submitted by the deadline that we agreed upon, and the final reports were not up to the standards we've agreed upon."

Often, we don't even realize that we've made a judgment when we are trying to provide feedback. It's important to think about how you convey your message beforehand to ensure that it is judgment-free. If your goal is to help mold or change employees' performance, leaving your judgments out of the conversation will help employees focus on their own behaviors rather than on what you think of them.

Evidence-based feedback is a tool that encourages self-assessment and accountability. It takes some thought to distinguish the facts from your judgments, but the results are more meaningful to employees and more productive for you. Conversations based on evidence lead to employees owning the situation because they can focus on the evidence you have presented rather than your judgment.

Let's Apply It

For each scenario listed in Table 6.2, determine whether the manager's feedback is a judgment or fact-based evidence. Suggested responses follow the exercise.

Table 6.2   Judgment or Evidence?

1. You did not share enough information with me. The next time you need to tell me everything so that I can make an informed decision.		2. After your presentation, one of the crewmembers said that your suggestions will make their jobs easier.	
▦ Judgment	▦ Evidence	▦ Judgment	▦ Evidence
3. I didn't like the way you handled that request. You could have done better.		4. Great job today! You were awesome at that presentation!	
▦ Judgment	▦ Evidence	▦ Judgment	▦ Evidence
5. Today you exceeded the goal for new cases established and are on target to exceed your monthly goal as well.		6. You asked good questions during the meeting.	
▦ Judgment	▦ Evidence	▦ Judgment	▦ Evidence
7. Your response led the customer to raise her voice and threaten to take her business elsewhere.		8. You said that the company is open to the customer's perspectives. When you said that, the customers began to share their ideas.	
▦ Judgment	▦ Evidence	▦ Judgment	▦ Evidence

9. When I asked you about the incident, you did not tell me that the fire department chose not to respond.		10. Your approach to the project offered numerous scenarios, which allowed the client to have a choice in the final design.	
▪ Judgment	▪ Evidence	▪ Judgment	▪ Evidence
11. You're consistently not following company policy.		12. You did not respond to two work orders that were due today.	
▪ Judgment	▪ Evidence	▪ Judgment	▪ Evidence

How did you do? Here is a quick summary of the correct answers to the exercise in Table 6.2.

1. *You did not share enough information with me. The next time you need to tell me everything so that I can make an informed decision.*

   Judgment. There are no specific examples to help the employee understand what he or she should have done differently in the situation. Without specific examples, or evidence, the employee is left with only your judgment. A better response is, "You did not share with me the feedback from the auditors. That was information that was relevant to our final decision."

2. *After your presentation, one of the crewmembers said that your suggestions will make their jobs easier.*

   Evidence. This is a statement of evidence to support that the employee did a good job.

3. *I didn't like the way you handled that request. You could have done better.*

   Judgment. Without specific examples or evidence to describe what happened, the employee is unclear as to how to improve. A better reply is, "When you responded to the client by saying that we couldn't supply the materials until Friday, it left the client without an alternative."

4. *Great job today! You were awesome at that presentation!*

    Judgment. Even though this is a positive statement about the quality of the employee's presentation, it includes no details that will help the employee repeat the performance. A more evidence-based response is, "When you asked the group to provide their ideas, you engaged them in your presentation."

5. *Today you exceeded the goal for new cases established and are on target to exceed your monthly goal as well.*

    Evidence. This is specific evidence of the employee's good work. It also provides data that will encourage the employee to continue performance at this level.

6. *You asked good questions during the meeting.*

    Judgment. "Good questions" does not help the employee know what or why the questions were effective. It's a judgment. A better statement would be, "When you asked about the number of returns we've received, it allowed the group to explore new and important territory."

Reflection Question

During the last performance-related conversation you had with an employee, did you offer evidence or judgment?

---

7. *Your response led the customer to raise her voice and threaten to take her business elsewhere.*

    Evidence. Regardless of whether the employee incited the customer's behavior, the statement is offered as judgment-free evidence. Presenting the situation in this way, without judgment, allows you and the employee to explore what really happened without your opinion getting in the way.

8. *You said that the company is open to the customer's perspectives. When you said that, the customers began to share their ideas.*

    Evidence. Restating the employee's words is a way to use evidence to reinforce good performance.

9. *When I asked you about the incident, you did not tell me that the fire department chose not to respond.*

Evidence. This is a statement of the facts. It does not include an immediate judgment about whether the employee was right or wrong.

10. *Your approach to the project offered numerous scenarios, which allowed the client to have a choice in the final design.*

   Evidence. Offering numerous scenarios provides evidence that the client had choices.

11. *You're consistently not following company policy.*

   Judgment. This statement contains a leap. It assumes the employee knows what behaviors are in question, and it links them to policies that are not explicitly stated. Offering a specific, fact-based example would be more effective. An example is, "You did not wear your safety goggles today. This is a violation of our company policy."

12. *You did not respond to two work orders that were due today.*

   Evidence. This is a verifiable fact that allows the employee to explore the details of the situation, rather than react to a judgment about his or her timeliness.

Painless Perspective

Separate your judgments from the evidence. Stick to evidence when initiating a performance conversation.

Focus on the Gap

When you've been clear about your expectations and the employee has behaved in a way that does not meet your expectations, your conversation can focus on that gap between the two, as illustrated in Figure 6.1, rather than the employee's defense against your judgment of the situation.

When you talk with an employee about performance and your intent is to help that employee improve, focusing on the gaps will keep the conversation judgment-free. By focusing on the gap, the conversation can target the facts, which allows you to focus on evidence rather than your judgment or conclusions about the employee.

Once you know that a gap exists between what you expect and what you have observed, the next step is to determine the reason for the gap. The

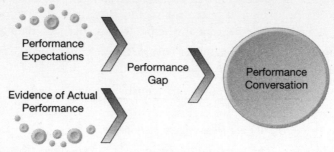

Figure 6.1   Performance Gap Model

best way to determine why there is a gap is to have a painless performance conversation with the employee to determine the causes. Hearing directly from the employee will lead you to a more successful outcome than jumping to conclusions about why the gap exists.

Let's Apply It

For each example in Table 6.3, identify the gap between what was expected and the actual performance.

Table 6.3   Identifying the Performance Gap

Performance Expectation	Actual Performance	Gap
At least five client files will be closed out each day.	Hannah has been closing an average of two to three client files each day for the past month.	The gap is the difference between closing three files and five files.
Voicemails and e-mails will be returned within 24 hours.	Brian has not returned at least five voicemails that were left on Monday, and he has 20 e-mails in his inbox that have not been responded to. It is Thursday.	

White papers should be prepared with complete research and full documentation of sources.	Gary's last two white papers have not included references and have not cited statistics.	
As teamwork is important, all employees are expected to jump in to help coworkers when there is a backlog in any one individual's queue.	Hudson completes his own assignments on time or early almost every day, but he has not offered to assist a coworker any time during the past month.	
Respect and courtesy is the basis upon which we interact in the office.	Lauren shouted profanities at Mitch and left the staff meeting abruptly after the incident. The staff meeting had not been adjourned when she left.	

During the conversation, you can come to a productive, painless conclusion if you present the evidence you have gathered, compare it with the expectation you have established, and seek the employee's input. After some dialogue, you will come to a conclusion with the employee and determine the next steps. Sounds easy, huh? Of course there are a few more details to consider.

Painless Perspective

Concentrate on the gap between actual performance and your clearly defined performance expectations.

What Creates Performance Gaps?

In a conversation with the employee you will explore several reasons for the performance gap. Here are several possibilities to consider:

- **The employee doesn't know what you expect**. You may believe that you've been clear with your expectations, but it's possible the employee sees a different goal. A gap can exist because you haven't given clear enough direction or because the job itself is not clearly defined.

*   *   *

- **The employee doesn't have the knowledge, skills, or abilities to meet your expectations**. If the employee is not getting it, he or she may need additional training, coaching, or support. The employee may be unable to deal with the pressures of the job or may be struggling to understand how the job fits into the bigger picture.

*   *   *

- **The employee doesn't want to meet your expectations**. If the employee has the knowledge, skills, and abilities to do the job or if the employee has performed it successfully in the past, the problem may be in that person's willingness to do the job. When the work changes, technology is introduced, or demands increase, the employee may experience a change in his or her level of commitment to the job. Your job is to identify this shift and address the gap through conversation.

The reality is in what a person cannot reveal to you.

—Kahlil Gibran

Closing the Gaps

As you discuss the gap between what you expect and what you have observed, you will begin to uncover the reasons for the gaps. Once the reason for the gap is clear, your options for closing the gap will become evident.

Consider these solutions to bridging gaps in employee performance.

- **The employee doesn't know what you expect**. When it's clear that the employee does not understand your expectations, you will have a number of options to pursue, including:

□ Update and agree on a more specific job description.

□ Set clear, appropriate goals and standards.

□ Provide active and frequent support as the employee performs the job.

□ Provide regular, structured feedback and coaching.

□ Delegate work in a more structured way.

* * *

■ **The employee doesn't have the knowledge, skills, or abilities to meet your expectations**. Employees are not likely to admit to you that they don't have the skills necessary to do the job. However, after questioning and exploring the cause of the problem, you may determine that an employee is indeed lacking in knowledge, skills, or abilities. To address this kind of a gap consider options such as:

□ Providing additional training

□ Further developing knowledge and skills through coaching

□ Giving frequent feedback as the employee performs the job

□ Seeking support from other team members

□ Considering temporary adjustments to duties or performance standards until the employee can perform the full functions of the job

* * *

■ **The employee doesn't want to meet your expectations**. Throughout your conversation with the employee, you will be exploring his or her perspectives on the performance gap. If it becomes apparent that the employee has the skills and knowledge to do the job and understands your performance expectations yet is still unwilling, the solution may be to address the employee's will. Again, your job is to ascertain whether the employee is willing to meet your expectations. Your job is not to make a judgment about the employee's willingness.

Keep in mind that there may be more than one underlying cause of a performance gap, and your focus must be on highlighting the evidence you have observed before moving to a solution. Painless performance conversations are the tool for identifying and closing the gaps.

Giving Better Feedback

Once you identify performance gaps, consider these additional suggestions for giving meaningful feedback:

- Focus on desired outcomes, identified skill gaps, and end results. When feedback is framed as a means to an end, it becomes an opportunity to solve a problem rather than an opportunity to criticize a person. Frame feedback around something that is critical to the work group, to the organization, and to the employee.

- Don't think you know it all. Remember, there are at least two sides to every story. Even if you think you know the facts, you might not have the complete story. Approach feedback conversations with the goal of getting a complete and accurate picture, which includes the employee's perspective. Be willing to listen and be influenced by what you hear.

- Give feedback quickly, frequently, and regularly. Feedback works more effectively when it is an ongoing activity rather than a formal event with the door closed. The more you offer it, formally and informally, as part of your daily management routine, the more feedback-friendly your work environment becomes.

- Feedback is not a one-and-done exercise. Just because you had a discussion about the employee's performance doesn't mean the conversation is over. The employee's ability to change his or her behavior may require ongoing support. Following up is vital. If you don't follow up, the employee may just "wait you out" until you raise the issue (and the stakes) again.

Conversation Checkpoints

- Employees want your feedback. They want to know what you think of their performance.

- Concentrate on the gap between what you expect and what you have observed.

- Separate feedback from judgments and provide feedback to employees to help them improve their performance.

- Giving feedback regularly creates an environment where employees expect and desire your input.

From the Field

From Tom, Software Development Manager:

I have managed the same group of five programmers for about four years. The team has been together for the same amount of time, and it's a cohesive group. After a recent restructuring of the organization, I inherited a new programmer from another division, and I think I need to intervene to help the new staff member get up to speed with the group's work.

I have noticed that the new programmer is less enthusiastic about the company's mission and the team's work than the other members of my team. The new staff member seems to have really low energy, is lethargic, and seems uninterested in bonding with his new teammates. He doesn't greet teammates when he arrives each morning, he eats lunch alone at his desk, and he hasn't spoken up at the weekly development meetings. I'm planning to bring these concerns to his attention, but I want to make sure I do it effectively. This seems like a conversation that could backfire pretty easily.

Sound Bites from the Field

Jumping to the conclusion that the new staff member is uninterested in bonding with his new teammates could backfire on Tom. The employee may have other perspectives to share about the work and the work group. To ensure the employee does not immediately get defensive, Tom might begin the conversation like this:

I've noticed that you haven't spoken up at the development meetings and that you are keeping to yourself most of the time. How are you feeling about working here? How is it going so far?

By stating the behavior he has observed and then allowing the employee to provide his perspective, Tom will avoid judging the employee and will allow room for the employee to participate in the conversation.

Lessons Learned from the Field

Tom must focus on the observable behaviors of the programmer rather than his conclusions about the employee's motivations. Although it is possible that the programmer is unenthusiastic about the new job, he may also be shy, reserved, or observing the environment before jumping in. He may be working to develop a relationship with his new colleagues before speaking up.

Tom can build rapport and discover how to create a motivating environment for the employee by stating the evidence he's observed and then allowing the employee to participate in the direction of the conversation. Along the way, Tom can be clear about his expectations related to team contributions and help the employee find ways to bridge the gap.

Next Up

In Chapter 7 you'll explore the third of the four painless performance conversation mind-sets: inquire with purpose. By framing the problem and asking questions that expand possibilities, you will be able to create an environment where the employee is involved in problem solving.

7 | Inquire with Purpose

Using Curiosity to Expand Possibilities

The effect that questioning has on the mind can be likened to the stimulus given to a fire by poking; it disturbs the settled arrangement and brings about new combinations.

—William Beveridge

Many managers take up too much space in their conversations with employees. They think they know the answers and that employees should listen. As a result, managers do all of the talking and employees are not presented with an opportunity to share their feelings or their side of the story. However, the best managers know it is the other way around.

To gain employee support and buy-in, great managers do more listening than talking. They ask questions, and they believe that others have good ideas to offer. The third critical mind-set of a painless performance conversation is to use your curiosity to help employees solve their own challenges.

You probably became a manager because you were really good at solving problems and completing work. You may have been promoted because you were technically competent. It makes sense that you should be able to tell others how to do the job because you were good at it. The problem: few employees want to be told what to do.

Because you are technically competent to do the job, it's easy to step into problem-solver mode. Yet, most employees want to be involved. Some warning signs that you are being a solver rather than an involver may be when you begin sentences with:

"You need to. . . . "
"You should. . . . "
"You'd be better off/more successful/happier if you would. . . . "
"Why don't you. . . . "

It may seem quicker and easier to tell employees what to do, but you won't gain their commitment. Instead, you gain commitment when you work toward agreement with them about problems and ask them to contribute to the solutions. Why would they want to do what you are telling them to do if they don't agree that a change needs to be made?

I have no special gift. I am only passionately curious.

—Albert Einstein

Asking more and telling less can be challenging. Here are three ideas to help you use questions to gain the support of your employees.

1. **Ask questions that show you care.** Rather than telling your staff that there is a problem that needs to be fixed, ask them what they think the problem is. When you listen, they will be more likely to offer up solutions they can endorse. Effective question asking opens the lines of communication and shows you care about their contributions. Simple questions such as, "How do you think we can solve this?" or "What ideas do you have?" signal to employees that you care.

2. **Ask questions that promote buy-in.** The next time an employee comes to you for advice, resist the temptation to give the answer. This is tough if you've "been there, done that." However, if you really want the employee to believe in the solution, ask what he or she thinks the best solution is. When involved in this way, the employee is more likely to support the outcome. Through effective questioning, great managers lead employees to their own solutions and afford their employees personal growth opportunities along the way. The easy way to do this is to ask a question such as, "What do you think?" before you give your suggestion.

3. **Zip it!** One of the most difficult things for motivated, high achievers is not to give their own opinions. However, this is the one skill that can help you build relationships faster than any other. After you ask questions of your employees, close your mouth, maintain eye contact, and wait for a response. Resist the tendency to give your own answer. A little bit of silence will go a long way.

Making Space in the Conversation

Imagine a conversation as if you and the employee are in a contained space, like a box. The more you talk, the more space you take up in the box. The more space you take up, the less room there is for the employee to contribute ideas, share perspectives, or even have his or her own ideas. When you ask questions and stop to listen to the employee's ideas, it creates more space for the employee, which means the employee can fully participate in the conversation. Making space for the employee is critical because it allows him or her to share insights and eventually own the outcome.

Painless Perspective

Instead of telling employees the answer, ask them what they think.

Respond in Question Marks

For many managers, it is easier to give answers than to ask questions. The expedient route may be to solve the employee's problem. However, when you jump straight to problem solving, you cheat yourself of fresh ideas from the employee—and you shift the burden back onto your own shoulders. When you respond with questions, the conversation can prepare the employee for greater independence, to explore new solutions, and to develop a deeper capacity on your team.

Asking employees for their ideas encourages them to think on their own. However, responding with questions may not lead to immediate employee engagement. So the more consistently you ask, the more likely employees will get involved in finding a solution.

You can tell employees all day long what they need to do and have minimal impact on their performance. For example, Sam wished his new intern would be more self-directed. When the intern finished a task, he'd come to Sam looking for the next assignment. Once that assignment was completed, he'd come back for another. Sam was frustrated by the frequent interruptions and wondered why the intern wouldn't show initiative and find work to do on his own.

Painless Perspective

The less you talk, the more effective you will be as a leader.

A well-placed, powerful question has the ability to shift an employee's focus faster than a day of lectures. What if, during one of those assignment-seeking interruptions from the intern, Sam would have stopped to ask, "What have you noticed lately that needs to get done around here that is just not getting done?" The intern may have some interesting and helpful ideas. Of course, Sam has to show patience and allow room in the conversation for the intern to respond. In this role, Sam's job is to encourage the employee to think and explore. If done with sincerity and true interest, he has the potential to shift the intern's thinking and truly change behavior. Although this collaborative approach takes more time initially, it will yield greater, longer-lasting results both for the intern and for the organization. It will also save Sam a great deal of time in the future.

In the case of Sam and the intern, Sam found that the intern had some innovative and cost-saving ideas for using technology to monitor workflow and to organize jobs. By stopping to ask one thought-provoking question, Sam opened the door to a conversation that engaged the intern and led to productivity enhancements.

Ask, Ask, Ask

Powerful questions take aim at the root of our assumptions and beliefs. Asking questions can help employees notice details and patterns they may have previously overlooked. The right question, at the right time, has the power to shift another's thinking in ways a monologue, even by the most gifted speaker, never could.

The most successful leaders drive their conversations with questions. Those who are most effective in leadership roles use questions more frequently than those who don't. Leaders are more successful when they ask questions rather share their own points of view.

Reflection Question

In your last conversation with an employee, what did you do more of: ask questions or give answers?

The curiosity that is fostered by asking questions also creates a culture of exploration and risk taking. When managers ask more questions, employees are more willing to challenge the status quo and try new approaches. To engage employees in problem solving and to increase their commitment to solutions, ask questions.

An important shift for leaders is to supplement their role of answer finder with the role of question asker.

—Charles J. Palus and David H. Horth

What to Ask

So, what should you ask? If you are not in the habit of being curious and are more likely to offer solutions without taking the time to help employees seek their own answers, try asking these two simple questions:

1. **How do you feel/think?** This is a great question to start with because you can tailor it to the person and the situation. For example, "How do you feel about the new process for managing the budget?" "What do you think about the new organizational structure?" "How do you feel the project is coming along?" "What do you think about the proposal?" Just start by asking how employees feel or what they think.

2. **What do you need?** By asking what an employee needs, you open the dialogue to possibilities. This easy question can also be adapted to any situation. For example, "What do you need to complete this task on time?" "What do you need to feel comfortable with our approach?" "What do you need to be satisfied with the outcome?" Seeking input about what the other person needs allows you to learn about how you can help while letting the employee know that you have an interest in his or her success.

To be able to ask a question clearly is two-thirds of the way to getting it answered.
—Sam Ruskin

Let's Apply It

For one week, spend at least 3 minutes each day in a conversation with an employee where you only ask questions and listen. Don't interject. Don't interrupt. Don't share your perspective. Just ask and listen. At the end of each conversation, ask yourself:

- What was it like to withhold your comments in order to listen to the employee's ideas?
- What was the outcome of the conversation?

If you are asking open-ended, thought-provoking questions, you are likely to leave the conversation with more information than you started with, while also enhancing goodwill between you and the employee.

The Power of Questions

A prudent question is one half of wisdom.

—Sir Francis Bacon

Questions can accomplish a lot. They create clarity. They lead to better working relationships. Really good questions help people think analytically and critically. Here are some questions that foster analysis:

- "What are the consequences of going this route?"
- "What are some other potential outcomes?"
- "What are the possible directions you might have considered?"

Questions inspire people to reflect and see issues in fresh, unpredictable ways. They encourage breakthrough thinking and new perspectives. A few thought-provoking questions include:

- "What other ways could this be accomplished?"
- "If money were no object, how would you approach this?"
- "What resources might it take to make this happen?"

These questions challenge the assumptions that all employees carry with them into the workplace. Instead of telling employees what *you* think they should do, try asking *them* for their thoughts with questions such as:

- "Based on your experience, what do you think we should do?"
- "What do you suggest in this situation?"
- "What options have you considered?"

Knowing how to probe for additional insights is a skill you can develop over time. The following list provides additional questions you can use to encourage employees to participate in a performance conversation:

Relationship-Building Questions
- What are your thoughts about . . . ?
- I'd like to hear your opinions about . . .

- What can I do to help?
- What do you need to be successful?

Information-Seeking Questions

- Please tell me more about . . .
- What are your ideas about . . . ?
- What if . . . ?
- What options have you considered?

Detail-Clarifying Questions

- What did you mean by . . . ?
- Could you give me an example of . . . ?
- Help me understand . . .
- Describe the situation for me from your unique perspective.

Interest-Defining Questions

- What is your ideal outcome?
- What was the reasoning behind . . .
- What other alternatives did you consider?
- What led you to that conclusion?
- What would you ideal outcome be?

Data-Gathering Questions

- Did you know that . . . ?
- Help me understand the difference between my information, which says____, and your information, which says____.
- Considering ____, tell me how you came to this conclusion.

Resolution-Seeking Questions

- How can we . . . ?
- What would you recommend?
- If you could . . . ?
- What is the outcome you would like to see?
- How might we best resolve this?
- In the perfect world, how would you . . . ?
- Considering the facts we've discussed, how can you . . . ?

Five Whys

Questions can also help employees have a deeper understanding of systems and processes. One of the practices initially established by the carmaker Toyota was to ask, "Why?" five times. For example, if an employee is working on a piece of machinery and cuts his finger, the first question to ask is, "Why did he cut his finger?" The answer might be, "Because he put his finger in the machine." In that case, the next question might be, "Why did he put his finger in the machine?" And that answer might be, "Because the machine wasn't functioning." The next logical question is, "Why wasn't the machine functioning?" The answer may be, "Because the oil had run dry." The next question is, "Why had the oil run dry?" And the next response might be, "Because the preventive maintenance hadn't been done on the machine as scheduled." The fifth question in the sequence would be, "Why hadn't the preventive maintenance been done?" This series of questions leads to conclusions that are probably much more powerful than just: "That guy shouldn't have stuck his finger in the machine." Really good questions help us think analytically and critically. In this case, the five why questions included:

1. Why did he cut his finger?
2. Why did he put his finger in the machine?
3. Why wasn't the machine functioning?
4. Why had the oil run dry?
5. Why hadn't the preventive maintenance been done?

In a nutshell, questions can provide value on multiple levels. In the short term, questioning helps us generate solutions to the problem at hand. In the long term, questioning gives employees the tools to handle similar issues in the future and to solve problems independently.

Reflection Question

How can you incorporate more questions into the conversations you have with employees?

Tell Me about It

When faced with an opportunity to have a conversation with an employee about performance, your first question will establish the tone and direction of the conversation. One way to start the conversation is to describe the issue from your perspective, and then just say, "Tell me about it."

Here's an example:

Mia, I've noticed you have a number of reports on your desk that were scheduled to be finished and turned in last week. *Tell me about it.*

Next, be quiet and listen. By asking and listening, you go right to the core of the issue. You're not clouding the situation with your emotions or your preconceived perspectives. You're just talking about what you've noticed. There is no assumption about what has happened. You've just noticed, and you want to hear the other person's point of view. In fact, you're taking the problem behavior and putting it on the employee's shoulders without placing blame or fault. You are simply saying what you have observed.

Here's another example:

Mike, I noticed that you and your crew seem to be at odds lately. *Tell me about it.*

By saying, "Tell me about it," you are opening the door to all kinds of possibilities. This approach provides room in the conversation for the other person to give you his or her perspective. There may be something going on that you didn't know about. The employee may share information you really need to know. You could hear, "I don't know. I don't think there's a problem." You might find that there really isn't an issue from that employee's perspective. Regardless of the employee's response, you have raised the issue and set the tone for an open exploration of the situation. Continue with more questions, including, "What are your perspectives?" and "What is your viewpoint on this issue?"

Painless Perspective

The truth is that you don't have all of the truth.

Here's one more example:

Marla, during the staff meeting, I noticed that you seemed unhappy with the direction we're going. You rolled your eyes and seemed to have an opinion you didn't share when we talked about restructuring. *Tell me about it.*

Again, you aren't telling the employee how to be. You are inviting conversation about how the employee is right now. Marla may say, "What do you mean? I didn't roll my eyes." Or she may say, "Yeah, I really think we're going down the wrong path." You might get a variety of responses from the employee when you clearly state what you've observed. Ask the employee to tell you more and listen.

Guidelines for Powerful Questions

Forming questions on the spot can be challenging. It's a skill that takes some practice to develop. Here are some tips for creating strong questions.

1. **Use the context of the situation to *paraphrase* what has been said and leverage that in a new direction.**

   There's no need to create defensiveness in the conversation, yet it's important to convey that the employee is responsible for addressing the issue. Paraphrasing is the first step to a powerful question. Here are some examples of what a paraphrase might sound like:

   You say that the workload has become too heavy and that it is unreasonable to expect you to complete all of the tasks in an 8-hour day. Can you give me some examples of what tasks are harder to accomplish recently?

   In another example:

   I know you have been struggling lately with Megan. You have had several conflicts, and now the two of you are not speaking. What do you think needs to happen for the two of you to get on productive working terms again?

By restating in your own words what the employee has said, you are confirming that you have listened. If your paraphrase is not correct in the employee's eyes (or ears), he or she will let you know and you can redirect your response. Paraphrasing is easy. Use your own words to tell the employee what you have heard and then follow with a question to direct the conversation where you need it to go.

2. **Make questions *open-ended*.**

   The concept of open-ended questions is simple. Open-ended questions can't be answered with a simple yes or no, and they usually invoke a more detailed or thoughtful response. They cannot be answered with one-word responses, and as a result, they usually lead to the employee sharing his or her thoughts. Essentially, open-ended questions allow for more possibilities and directions for the conversation.

   Closed-ended questions, on the other hand, can be answered with a single one- or two-word response, often a yes or no. They don't leave room for elaboration, interpretation, or opinion. To encourage employee engagement and participation in problem solving, it's important to ask open-ended questions. Here are a few examples:

   "Do you like your work?" is closed-ended. You are likely to get a short, blunt, or yes or no answer to this question. An open-ended, alternative is, "What about your work do you most enjoy?" The response is more likely to be robust enough to give you insights into the employee's motivations.

   "Are you going to make that mistake again?" is closed-ended and will likely put the employee on the defensive. It is parental in nature and does not allow the employee to participate in solving the problem. An open-ended alternative would be, "What could you do next time to make sure the outcome is more effective?"

3. **Use *plural nouns* to open or expand the other person's options.**

   The more options available, the more in control the employee will feel. When asking questions to involve employees in problem solving, use plural nouns to extend the employees' perspectives and options. A plural noun is a word that is used to describe more than one object, place, person, or thing. For example, plural nouns used in a performance conversation might include *ideas, concerns, suggestions,* or *thoughts.*

   Plural nouns encourage the employee to consider multiple options and convey your openness to unique approaches. It encourages the employee to think of more than one solution.

   Plural nouns used in your open-ended questions might include words such as:

- □ *Goals* rather than *goal*
- □ *Options* rather than *option*
- □ *Perspectives* rather than *perspective*
- □ *Ideas* rather than *idea*
- □ *Alternatives* rather than *alternative*

For example:

What **options** have you considered to meet the customer's needs?

What **perspectives** can you share about your experience with the project?

What **ideas** do you have for solving the problem?

The singular nouns in these examples (*option, perspective, idea*) limit the response you will receive and do not encourage the employee to participate in the resolution of the issue.

4. **Frame the question with *your boundaries*.**

You may be tempted to avoid asking questions if you are uncertain what the answers will be. One way to encourage dialogue while still maintaining control of the direction of the conversation is to use boundaries to frame the issue. Boundaries allow you to acknowledge conditions in your environment that are:

- □ Constraints
- □ Limitations
- □ Agreements
- □ Expectations
- □ Beyond your control
- □ Current realities
- □ Nonnegotiable factors

The frame of your question creates parameters that define the givens. These are the assumptions you have already made that are nonnegotiable. Such factors might include your budget, the economy, the current staffing levels, the mission of the group, the vision for the future, the technology currently available, or your expectations for performance. Anything that defines current reality can serve as a frame for a question. Here are a few examples:

- □ *Given our current budget situation,* which of our projects is the highest priority?
- □ *Assuming we will meet our end-of-the-year objectives,* what additional goals should we pursue?

◻ *Knowing that our relationship with this client is tenuous and our goal is to strengthen the relationship,* what options do we have for satisfying this order?

◻ *Given the restrictions placed on us in the state statute,* what alternatives should be considered?

◻ *Considering that the machine is broken and replacement parts won't be delivered for seven days,* what options do we have for maintaining production?

5. **Use exploratory language to encourage new thoughts and viewpoints.**

Exploratory language conveys to the employee that you're open to possibilities. Words that are exploratory include:

◻ Might

◻ If

◻ Could

◻ Consider

◻ Possibly

◻ Maybe

◻ Perhaps

Examples of these words in play include:

◻ "What *might* be the possible outcomes of that approach?"

◻ "*If* the funding is approved, what priorities *could* you focus on?"

◻ "*Perhaps* we *could consider* a few additional options. What alternatives have you identified?"

Painless Perspective

Ask questions that invoke the employee's perspective. Frame the issue and stimulate new thinking and exploration.

Putting It All Together

Effective management always means asking the right question.

—Robert Heller

Powerful and purposeful questions are an integral part of engaging employees in a conversation about finding solutions to issues that you don't

Figure 7.1 Creating Engaging Questions

need to resolve on your own. Using the five guidelines for powerful questions, follow this easy process, illustrated in Figure 7.1, for creating questions that get employees involved.

Here are a few examples of how questions can be used to stoke the fires of creativity with your employees.

Employee: There are so many changes going on right now. I don't see how you can expect us to keep up with all the work we are facing.

Manager: *(paraphrase)* So you are concerned about keeping up with the increasing workload. *(frame)* As we both know, change is constant in our industry. Our resources are shrinking while demand from our customers continues to grow. *(open-ended question with plural nouns)* What options do we have as a work unit to adjust to our shifting priorities?

* * *

Employee: I just don't know how you think I'm going to meet these goals, considering the lack of support I've been receiving from the folks in purchasing.

Manager: *(paraphrase)* Our department's relationship with the purchasing function has been a challenge to meeting our objectives in the past. *(frame)* That hurdle doesn't change the fact that we are all expected to meet our quarterly goals and work together. *(open-ended question with plural nouns)* What ideas do you have for building a stronger relationship with purchasing so that you can more effectively get your work completed on time?

* * *

Employee: It just seems like we continue to work hard, but the results are not as good as they used to be. It's frustrating because we are not producing as much as we did last year, but we're working just as many hours.

Manager: *(paraphrase)* The current business climate has made our work more difficult. *(frame)* We cannot continue to use the same old methods and expect them to produce the same results in the future. *(open-ended question with plural nouns)* What new strategies might we consider to boost our effectiveness?

Conversation Checkpoints

- Asking questions is the most effective way to engage employees in painless performance conversations and thus solve workplace problems.
- Effective questioning requires you to listen actively and to be open to the employee's perspective.
- Questions can enhance clarity of understanding, build relationships, define other's interests, and seek resolution. They make space in the conversation.
- Ask, "Why?" five times to get to the real answer.
- An effective question begins with a paraphrase, includes a frame of the boundaries, and presents an open-ended perspective with multiple options for answering.

From the Field

From Kristy, Law Enforcement Manager:

As a new manager to the organization, I was still learning the perspectives and styles of each of my employees. I knew that several employees were struggling to keep pace with the workload and one of the most challenged employees was Judi. Judi and I had spoken several times about the declining quality of her work. I was surprised when she came to me to discuss the workload.

Judi shared with me that she was very concerned about the staffing reductions we'd experienced over the past few years. Judi said that she wanted to do a good job but felt that it was impossible to do so with the current level of resources. Judi talked about the way it was, "back in the day," when staffing was almost double what it is now.

I wanted to tell Judi that she needed to work harder. I wanted to use the conversation to let her know that the work was not going to get easier and she was the one who needed to step it up. However, I knew that if I demanded a higher level of performance, the conversation would likely backfire.

Instead, I listened to Judi's perspective about the current workload and asked her a variety of questions to lead her to her own conclusion. In the end, Judi acknowledged that the environment was not likely to change in the near future and that she was going to have to rethink how she does her work. I could see that she was beginning to picture the new reality and what it would take for her to be successful in it.

Sound Bites from the Field

During the conversation with Judi, Kristy framed her questions with the current reality facing the organization. Part of their conversation sounded like this:

Kristy: Judi, the downsizing process has been tough on everyone. We've lost staff, and it's unlikely that those positions will be refilled. Given that staffing levels are not predicted to grow, what ideas do you have for meeting our increasing demand?

Judi: Oh, I don't know. I guess I'll just need to suck it up and work harder.

Kristy: We are all going to have to find new ways of doing our work. Knowing that the job is unlikely to change, what can you do to adapt to the new workload?

Judi: I don't know. There's just so much of it. I think we just need more people.

Kristy: Considering that increased staffing is not an option right now, what other options have you considered?

Judi: Hmm . . . I'm wondering if there are some tasks that are just not going to get done anymore. For example, my weekly summary report takes a lot of time to prepare, and I wonder if it's useful to anyone anymore.

Kristy: There may be certain tasks that take a lot of your time and were helpful in the past but are not essential now. The weekly summary may be one of those tasks. What else have you considered?

Judi struggled to come up with productive answers to some of the questions. Eventually, though, she shared several productive ideas that would begin to alleviate the pressure.

Lessons Learned from the Field

Kristy effectively used questions to guide Judi to an understanding that the work environment and the expectations for performance would remain unchanged. She also made it clear that Judi was responsible for identifying steps for adapting to the new environment.

The open-ended, thought-provoking questions posed by Kristy provided a spark that led Judi to consider new options. In the end, Judi was more willing to let go of tasks when she came up with the idea herself.

Next Up

In Chapter 8 you'll explore the last of the four painless performance conversation mind-sets: be clear. When you are clear about who owns the problem and who is responsible for taking steps for solving the issue, you enhance levels of accountability in your work environment.

8

Be Clear

Creating a Culture of Ownership

Peak performance begins with your taking complete responsibility for your life and everything that happens to you.

—Brian Tracy

Accountability. As a manager you may think you are expected to hold employees accountable for their performance. But what does it really mean to be accountable? Will holding employees accountable really make them more effective? Painless performance conversations focus on creating a culture of ownership, which is an employee-driven outcome, rather than holding employees accountable, which is a manager-directed activity. The fourth critical mind-set of a painless performance conversation is to create a culture of ownership by being clear about who is responsible for resolving the issue. Enhanced levels of ownership naturally lead to enhanced levels of accountability in the workplace.

Moving Beyond Accountability

When employees lack accountability, it usually means they are:

- Not meeting the performance expectations of the job
- Not recognizing or admitting their role in mistakes or problems
- Not demonstrating the organization's core values
- Not willing to learn from challenging situations
- Showing low morale and, likely, low self-esteem
- Not owning of their projects and assignments
- Not concerned about the impact of their work on others or on the organization

---

Painless Perspective

Foster ownership rather than demand accountability.

Work environments that demand accountability don't usually feel very good. Employees blame one another for problems, point fingers at management, and shift responsibility for finding solutions. High-performance/high-impact employees don't usually stay very long in these environments, feeling that their hard work is not valued.

Many researchers have tried to define the concept of accountability. The US Office of Personnel Management defines *accountability* as "being held answerable for accomplishing a goal or assignment." *Webster's Dictionary* says *accountability* is "subject to having to report, explain, or justify, or being answerable or responsible."

What's the common denominator in these common definitions? They imply guilt or fault. Accountability in these examples evokes blame. When employees are blamed, their automatic reaction is to be defensive, to come up with excuses, or to point fingers. Blame is not the pathway to a successful, thriving organization.

When you blame others, you give up your power to change.

—Unknown

In addition to being blame-focused, the traditional approach to account-ability is past-focused. In these conversations, the focus is on what has already happened and who is responsible for the outcome. The approach is negative, focusing on who is at fault.

In contrast, painless performance conversations are future-focused, exploring what will happen next. Moving forward, rather than looking backward, you and the employee are able to avoid the pain that comes from the blame. Focusing ahead, rather than on the past, the employee is more likely to want to be part of the conversation. As a result, he or she is more likely to own the solution, which leads to an engaged, motivated employee.

For example, if Bo's sales volume is below the expected quota and you tell him that he will be held accountable if the numbers do not increase, Bo is likely to react with fear, defensiveness, or resentment. His performance will probably not improve. However, if you have a conversation with Bo about his sales volume, exploring what he is planning to do in the future to increase his numbers, he is more likely to feel engaged and empowered to improve his performance. Blaming him for the poor results won't improve his perform-ance in the future.

A man can fail many times, but he isn't a failure until he begins to blame somebody else.

—John Burroughs

Let's Apply It

Complete Table 8.1, describing a recent performance-related conversation you have had with an employee. Explore the approach you used to discuss the performance issue.

Table 8.1 Your Performance Conversation

With whom did you have a performance conversation?	What issue or issues were addressed?	What was the employee's reaction?	Did the conversation focus on the past or on the future?	How did you contribute to the employee's reaction?

An Alternative to Accountability

Accountability is one of the worst best practices in business today, according to author Susan Scott. In her book *Fierce Leadership,* Scott suggests that "most of us associate accountability with blame, culpability, being wrong, maybe even being fired." Trying to hold people accountable creates an environment of fear, which naturally leads to a culture where employees are less likely to speak up, take risks, or be innovative. Holding employees accountable in the traditional sense is a bad idea and doesn't produce optimal results. If you can't hold employees accountable, what can you do to create greater levels of performance in the workplace?

Leadership is the art of getting someone else to do something you want done because he wants to do it.

—Dwight D. Eisenhower

An Alternative Approach: Ownership

As discussed, rather than past-focused accountability, shift your perspective to one that focuses more on the future, expecting employees to fully own the outcome of their efforts.

Ownership is choosing to take full responsibility for your behaviors, embracing the full result of your efforts regardless of the outcome, while focusing on how the future will improve because of your efforts.

Accountability is often done *to* employees. Ownership, on the other hand, represents the way in which employees engage in the world around them. Simply put, when employees own their work, accountability is the result.

With this definition of *ownership,* performance conversations are productive and forward thinking. The goal of a performance conversation is to help the employee leave the conversation knowing what he or she needs to do to solve the problem or improve performance. Rather than focusing on what you *don't* want to see, an ownership-focused conversation will focus on what the employee will do to enhance performance. Table 8.2 is a comparison of the concepts of accountability and ownership.

There is no contest between the company that buys the grudging compliance of its workforce and the company that enjoys the enterprising participation of its employees.

—Ricardo Semler

Table 8.2   A Culture of Ownership

From Accountability	To Ownership
Blame	Responsibility
Doing the job	Achieving results
Externalizing the cause	Internalizing the need to change
Working in silos	Collaborating with others
Telling others what to do	Engaging hearts and minds
Waiting for direction	Initiating change
Following along	Leading the way

Establishing a Culture of Ownership

As a manager, one of your roles is to create a culture of ownership. Establishing a culture of ownership is directly related to the clarity of your expectations. If you have established clear, tangible expectations for performance by defining an overall mission, values, and measurable outcomes, employees have a greater chance of meeting and/or exceeding those expectations.

Here is an example of ownership in action. For an employee on the pavement crew, a successful job is a filled pothole. Your expectation, however, is that the potholes be repaired so that they do not recur. If a pavement crew fills a pothole and the pothole comes back during the next week's rains, the crew hasn't achieved the expected results. Just because the pothole was filled once doesn't mean the job was completed if the hole keeps recurring.

Painless Principle

Focus on what you can control: the future. Let go of what you can't: the past.

In a culture of ownership, employees look for sustainable solutions by collaborating because they depend on others in the organization to achieve the expected results. Let's assume that the pothole is recurring with each rainfall because the Water Department has been working on the pipes under the street; as a result, the pothole keeps returning. If the hole keeps coming back, an appropriate solution won't be found in blaming another department for the problem.

An ownership culture is one where collaboration is used to solve the tough issues. If employees are truly accountable for results and your expectations are clear, they will be motivated to work across department lines to resolve the recurring pothole. A sure sign of ownership in this case would be for the pavement crew to contact the Water Department crew to collaborate on solutions that will prevent the pothole from recurring. In doing so, the employees engage their hearts and minds to find a solution, rather than blaming the other department.

Reflection Question

What opportunities exist to create greater levels of ownership within your team?

Tips for Engaging Employees' Hearts and Minds

How can you begin to establish a culture of ownership that engages employees' hearts and minds? Here are a few practical tips:

- Share big-picture and organizational plans early and often.
- Enlist employee participation in goal setting for the work unit.
- Conduct regular "keep interviews"—conversations about what will keep the employee motivated, engaged, and retained.
- Give employees ample opportunity to own their assigned projects and progress.
- Communicate reasonable expectations and check with employees to make sure they are clear on those expectations.
- Give frequent and immediate feedback so employees know when they are meeting your expectations.
- Give specific and timely feedback when employees are not meeting your expectations.
- Ask employees to make recommendations for addressing ongoing organizational challenges.
- Seek customer feedback and share it directly with employees in a timely manner.
- Break away from micromanaging. Set expectations and allow space for employees to learn. Learn to let go.
- Create a reward system to reinforce ownership behavior.

Creating the Hook

Helping employees own the outcome of their actions is a challenging proposition, especially for managers who are used to being in control. Sometimes, managers create an environment that lacks accountability simply through their daily conversations. When you respond to an employee in a way that lets the employee off the hook for his or her actions, you contribute to an environment that creates a lack of ownership.

For example, here's a conversation where the manager lets the employee off the hook:

Manager: Cory, it appears that you and John have been struggling to keep up with the demand for service lately.

Cory: No, that's not really the problem. John and I just don't get along. When he speaks at staff meetings, it just drives me crazy. That guy can't stay focused.

Manager: It sounds like you and John are having conflicts. Would it help if I talked with him and told him that he needs to get to the point quicker? If he would get to the point, you could better keep up with the demand for service.

This response takes the responsibility for addressing the problem off of Cory and leaves the burden for solving the issue with the manager.

Here's another way managers often respond that does not promote ownership:

Manager: If you're having conflicts with John, you should let him know that you need him to make his point more quickly. Likewise, he should let you know if he's not getting what he needs. The two of you need to work together to be able to keep up with the demand for service.

In this case the manager is telling the employee how to solve the problem. The response does nothing to prepare the employee to solve the issue himself. In both cases the manager let Cory off the hook. A better approach, which leaves the responsibility for the solution on the employee's shoulders, is to indicate that the employee owns the problem and is expected to identify a solution. It might sound like this:

Manager: It sounds like you and John are having trouble working together and that is affecting your ability to keep up with the demand for service. What steps can you take to resolve the conflicts you are having with John so that you can keep up with demand?

Another approach, which establishes clear expectations and leaves room for the employee to develop multiple options is:

Manager: The conflicts you are having with John can't continue. It's affecting your ability to keep up with the demand for service. I know you and John can resolve this issue. What options have you considered?

Both of these responses put the issue back onto the employee's shoulders. They indicate that the manager wants the behavior to change and doing so will improve service delivery. The manager is there to support the employee but will not resolve the issue for him. In this case, the employee owns the solution to the problem, thus creating an enhanced level of accountability within the work environment.

Painless Perspective

Employees must own the problem before they can own the solution.

Here are some examples of how managers often let employees off the hook and therefore take the ownership away, along with an alternative response that fosters ownership.

Off the Hook

> **Employee:** The data collection part of this project is really causing me trouble. If it keeps going in this direction, I'm afraid we won't be able to finish on time.
>
> **Manager:** You're right. This is a challenging project. I can show you how to do the data collection because that's the hardest part.

Ownership Response

> **Employee:** The data collection part of this project is really causing me trouble. If it keeps going in this direction, I'm afraid we won't be able to finish on time.
>
> **Manager:** This is a challenging project. Once you get through the data collection, however, the finish line will be near. What resources do you need to be able to get the data collection completed?

* * *

Off the Hook

Employee: It looks like we've got almost everything done for the graduation. I'm not sure what we are missing.

Manager: Well, I assume you'll be ordering certificates for everyone, and I haven't seen a request for those come through yet. Also, don't forget to check with Sara in Receiving to make sure the plaques are in stock. Oh, and don't forget . . .

Ownership Response

Employee: It looks like we've got almost everything done for the graduation. I'm not sure what we are missing.

Manager: Well, tell me about what you've done so far.

Employee: I've ordered the food, verified the list of graduates, and have checked with Receiving to make sure the plaques are in stock.

Manager: What's left to do?

Employee: Hmmm . . . oh, I almost forgot to order certificates!

Manager: Good thinking.

Off the Hook

Employee: In this case, we're juggling a lot of opinions. It's hard to know which perspectives are most critical.

Manager: Based on my experience, I'd make sure to call Alice and Elaine. They are really the most important people in this case.

Ownership Response

Employee: In this case, we're juggling a lot of opinions. It's hard to know which perspectives are most critical.

Manager: Whose perspectives are you considering?

Employee: I was thinking that Alice and Elaine probably have the greatest insights into this case.

Manager: They are certainly most aware of the issues. Anyone else you are thinking of talking with?

*   *   *

Off the Hook

> **Employee:**   I know I should check in with Mickie before we make this deal. I'm just dreading it because I'm afraid she's going to put up barriers to us moving forward.
> **Manager:**   Initiating a conversation with Mickie on this topic could be challenging. Would it help if I talked to her for you?

Ownership Response

> **Employee:**   I know I should check in with Mickie before we make this deal. I'm just dreading it because I'm afraid she's going to put up barriers to us moving forward.
> **Manager:**   Discussing this issue with Mickie could be challenging. How will you prepare for the meeting with her?

Delegating Back

It's easy to hand the ownership for solving a problem to the employee, and it's just as easy for the employee to hand it right back to you. Beware of reverse delegation. Employees who are unsure how to solve an issue may enlist you for help in solving it for them. Be careful not to automatically solve problems or make decisions for hesitant employees. Focus on generating alternative solutions together, making sure employees maintain responsibility for executing those solutions. When employees make statements such as, "You'll do a better job with this," or "You have so much more experience with these issues," they are delegating back to you. Although flattering, and possibly even true, these comments are often a way to get you to resolve an issue when it is really the employee's problem to solve. When employees are able to solve the problem today, they will be more independent tomorrow.

Here's an example of a conversation where the employee tries to shift ownership of the problem back to the manager and the manager responds by handing the ownership right back to the employee:

> **Manager:**   I understand the contract between the Shoemaker Corporation and our legal departments hasn't been finalized. What's the latest?
> **Employee:**   Legal is really dragging their feet. I keep leaving messages for Rebecca, but she doesn't return my calls. It's beginning to frustrate me.

Manager: What ideas have you considered for getting the process moving toward a conclusion?

Employee: Well, maybe you could call Legal and put some pressure on them. If you talked directly to Mike, maybe he can get Rebecca moving.

Manager: That's one solution. If we go that direction, you won't have uncovered the true reason for the delay. What other ideas do you have for getting a response from Rebecca?

Employee: I don't know. I was hoping you would just exert some muscle.

Manager: Closing this contract is your responsibility, and when it's done, the success will be the result of your effort. I know you can get this moving. What else could you do to get what you need from Rebecca?

Employee: I guess I could schedule a meeting with her to see if we can come to a resolution that way. E-mails don't seem to be working.

Manager: Good idea. Anything else?

Employee: I could try one more time to send an e-mail . . . or maybe I could give her a call early in the morning. I know she gets in pretty early.

Manager: Okay, let's try that. I'm sure if you continue to follow up you'll be able to get the response you need. Let's touch base on Friday to see what kind of progress you have made.

One of the greatest challenges of coaching (or teaching or parenting) is to realize that the ultimate motivation for change has to come from the person being coached—not the coach.

—Marshall Goldsmith

When you foster a work environment that values ownership, great things can happen, including:

- Improved levels of employee performance
- Enhanced engagement and enthusiasm
- Increased feelings of being valued
- Increased commitment and loyalty to the work and to the organization
- Higher levels of pride and ownership in the work product and the bottom line
- Improved safety and fewer accidents

- Reduced turnover
- More creativity and innovation
- Greater morale
- Greater job satisfaction

Rather than imposing solutions on the employee, use conversations that help the employee identify his or her own solutions that will improve performance and create an ownership culture.

Painless Perspective

You can't hold employees accountable and expect to create an environment of ownership, trust, and loyalty.

Conversation Checkpoints

- The traditional definition of *accountability* assigns blame and is therefore unproductive.
- *Ownership* means you are helping employees take full responsibility for problems and solutions.
- In a culture of ownership, employees internalize the need for change and act upon it willingly.
- Managers create a lack of ownership by letting employees off the hook.
- Allowing employees to delegate back to you takes responsibility away from the employee.

From the Field

From David, Information Technology Manager:

When I first hired Bill, I was hopeful that he was going to be my newest superstar. He was hired from a well-known software giant and came with more certifications than anyone I had ever met. That's why I was really hesitant to address the quality of his work when the problems began to pop up.

Although Bill was a sharp guy, he rarely produced a program that worked the way the customer requested. His output was functional, but the feedback we were getting was that Bill's work product was awkward or convoluted. When I shared the customer feedback with Bill, he always had a reason why the program needed to function the way it was designed and he was resistant to making changes. His responses gave the team and me few options for addressing the customer's concerns.

Finally, after one of our best customers complained yet again about a system enhancement that Bill created, I knew I needed to take a new approach. After all, we pride ourselves on having highly satisfied customers.

In the past I had respected his experience and begrudgingly taken his message back to the customer. This time I responded by letting him know that he was responsible for not just the coding but the customer's satisfaction with the end result. I made it clear that if the customer was not satisfied, Bill had not been successful.

Sound Bites from the Field

When David shared the latest customer concerns with Bill, the conversation went like this:

Bill: Considering the complexity of the system and the constraints we're facing, it's just not possible to do what the customer is asking. You'll have to tell them they are going to have to live with it the way it is.

David: Bill, this request is critical to our relationship with this customer. Considering the system constraints and the fact that we must finish this job with complete customer satisfaction, what options have you considered?

Bill (pushing back a bit): I've considered every avenue available. We just can't do it.

David: I know you've put a lot into this system, and we're at about 98 percent. Success is in the final 2 percent, and as the programmer, it's your job to find the 2 percent. What ideas do you have?

Bill: I just don't think it can be done. They are going to have to live with it.

David: This is the toughest part of our job—the final polish. If you don't address these issues, your job is not complete. So what options might you consider?

Bill: I guess I could go back to the code once more. Or maybe I could check with my online user database to see if anyone else has run up against this issue.

David: Good ideas, Bill. I believe there is a solution, and I know you can find it.

Lessons Learned from the Field

David felt as if he needed to respect Bill's experience and training. In fact, David did not have the technical expertise that Bill brought to the job. At the same time, he knew that customer satisfaction was the ultimate goal. By restating the desired end result and by not letting Bill off the hook, he made it clear that Bill was responsible for solving the issue. David defined his expectations related to the end product, that the customer's satisfaction was the ultimate goal. Regardless of how Bill resolved the issue, the end result had to be customer satisfaction. By being clear with his expectations and not allowing Bill to redirect the outcome, David reinforced a culture of ownership. In the end, Bill identified two simple changes that made the system acceptable to the customer.

Next Up

Establishing and communicating clear expectations and applying the four mind-sets is the foundation for having painless performance conversations. In Chapter 9 you'll explore the three critical elements of painless performance conversations and apply a simple format for leading performance conversations with confidence.

9 | Show Confidence

Conducting the Conversation

Each person's life is lived as a series of conversations.

—Deborah Tannen

Initiating and guiding a performance-related conversation can be intimidating. Feeling apprehensive and nervous is normal. Making sure to keep the conversation on track, maintain focus, and move forward productively can leave even the most experienced manager feeling a little incompetent. Because the outcome of the conversation is uncertain and because you never really know how the employee will respond, it's common to feel a little uneasy when entering into a performance conversation.

You can ease the uncertainty and lower your stress by having a plan for the conversation, being clear about your intended goal, and using the four mind-sets of a painless performance conversation. Doing so allows you to shift the responsibility for the outcome of the conversation to the employee. Ultimately, a painless performance conversation is one where you are:

- Separating actions from attitudes
- Focusing on performance evidence
- Using curiosity to expand possibilities
- Creating a culture of ownership

Applying the skills presented in the previous chapters in a thoughtful, structured way will help you achieve success. The purpose of this chapter is to provide a road map for those critical performance conversations.

Location, Location, Location

Place, time, and setting all send a critical message to the employee that the conversation is important. How you orchestrate the environment conveys the seriousness of the situation and your commitment to the issue.

What is the ideal location for a performance conversation? Here are a few options:

- In your office with the door closed
- In a conference room with the blinds and the door closed
- In the hallway
- In the car while driving
- At Starbucks over coffee
- In a location/meeting room that is free of distractions
- Outside in the fresh air

More than 50 percent of managers surveyed said they prefer to hold performance conversations in their office with the door closed. It's true that performance conversations need to be conducted in an environment that is free of distraction. The event needs to be taken seriously. However, take caution. Meeting in your office or in a conference room with the door closed may lead to the principal's office syndrome. This syndrome occurs when you invite employees to your office and close the door only when there is a problem. The closed door becomes a symbol that says trouble. Even if the door is only closed to discuss performance problems, it is perceived as a symbol of bad news and creates an environment of fear and distrust.

To avoid principal's office syndrome, consider having performance conversations at any time during the day and in almost any place. Performance conversations can take place anywhere you and the employee are able to focus on the issue. That location may be in the hallway if the conversation is going to be quick, or it may be over coffee. Depending on how in-depth the conversation is going to be, and whether you think the employee will need time to process the message, you may want to be in a private space.

Painless Perspective

The best location for a performance conversation is wherever you and the employee can focus.

Ultimately, get in the habit of having frequent performance conversations in a variety of environments. Eventually, employees will come to expect feedback from you—positive, constructive, or neutral—at any time, in any location. Here are some examples:

- As you are passing the employee in the hallway, say, "Hey, I've noticed your time cards were late last week," to bring the issue to his or her attention.
- As you and the employee are driving to a customer meeting say, "I'm concerned about the training budget and would like to talk with you about how you are planning to manage the cuts."
- As you and the employee are leaving a staff meeting, ask, "Do you have a few minutes to chat about yesterday's client presentation?"

Reflection Questions

Reflect back on your last performance conversation with an employee. Did you:

- Select an appropriate location?
- Pick a time when both you and the employee could focus on the conversation?
- Identify your intended outcome for the meeting?
- Eliminate distractions, including ringing phones, e-mail, text messages, prying eyes, and other people?

A Development State of Mind

Performance conversations require a development state of mind. This means you start the conversation with the intent to influence the growth and development of the other person. Ultimately, you have a performance conversation with an employee for one reason: to reinforce or change that person's behavior. Employees are more likely to listen and participate in the conversation when your intent is to help rather than to scold. When your goal is to develop the employee's skills, you set yourself and the employee up for long-term success. When you are committed to helping the employee improve performance, your frame of mind will influence the direction of the conversation. A development state of mind generates an environment where learning and improvement are possible. Your state of mind will also lead the employee to explore a wider variety of options for solving workplace problems.

Let's Apply It

To lead a conversation with the intent of helping and developing the employee requires you to hold some important beliefs about employees and their abilities. Before you initiate a performance conversation, check your current state of mind. Are the following true?

(continued)

> *(continued)*
>
> - I'm raising this concern for the employee's benefit.
> - I am trying to help the employee, while helping the organization.
> - This is a legitimate business issue rather than a personal pet peeve.
> - I am willing to travel a long road to resolve this issue with the employee.
> - If I avoid this conversation, the problem will persist.
> - I am clear about what we can accomplish in this conversation.
> - I am willing to work with the employee to find a mutually agreeable solution.
> - There may be multiple right answers to resolve this issue.
> - It's possible that I don't have all the answers.
> - I am willing to facilitate the employee's learning so that he or she can find workable solutions.
> - I realize that we may not resolve this issue in one conversation.
> - I understand the implications of the issue not being resolved and what steps I will take if the conversation is not successful.

If the preceding are true, you are in a development state of mind and ready to help the employee improve performance.

No man would listen to you talk if he didn't know it was his turn next.

—E.W. Howe

Three Essential Elements of a Painless Performance Conversation

A painless performance conversation is defined by three essential elements. Your goal is to lead the conversation so that the three elements illustrated in Figure 9.1 are present.

Let's explore each of these elements in more detail.

1. **There should be no surprises.** No one wants to be surprised when it comes to a work-related conversation. You can avoid surprises by being clear about your expectations and reinforcing them as often as possible.

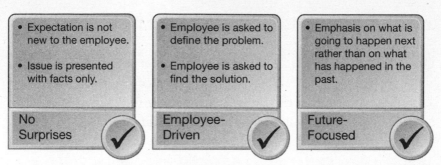

Figure 9.1   Elements of a Painless Performance Conversation

When you are clear about what you stand for and an employee doesn't live up to the expectations, there's no surprise that you will be having the conversation with that employee. Bringing up a concern when you have not been clear about your expectations will likely lead to surprise.

You can also avoid the surprise factor when you present the issue in factual terms. Begin the conversation by focusing on the specific details, which the employee most likely is aware of anyway. Do not make assumptions about how the employee feels or guess at why the employee did what he or she did. Do not bring up the past or other issues not central to your current concern. Too many details can dilute the effectiveness of your conversation. Begin with the facts at hand to avoid surprising the employee.

2. **The employee must solve the problem.** The employee must be responsible for finding a solution. Your job is to help the employee find a solution to which he or she can commit. Ask open-ended questions that encourage the employee to suggest alternatives and options for addressing the issue. By encouraging the employee to personally solve issues, you are fostering a culture of ownership. This may involve delegating back to the employee if he or she tries to persuade you to take on the issue.

3. **The focus remains on the future.** You are raising the issue because you believe that the employee can and will do something differently in the future. You realize that neither you nor the employee can change the past, so the focus of the conversation should be on what the employee will be doing in the future. You will also explore opportunities to reinforce the behavior once the employee has made the changes you have agreed upon. Focus forward.

It's a poor sort of memory that only works backwards, the Queen remarked.

—Lewis Carroll

The Painless Performance Conversation Model

Using the painless performance conversation model will allow you and the employee to downshift for a moment—to focus on a common goal and options. The model is structured to encourage the employee to find the answers and own the outcome. When you begin a performance-related conversation, consider this model for keeping the meeting focused and productive.

Step 1: Explain the situation and why the issue is important.
- State the facts.
- Explain the impact of the situation on the organization.
- Be concise!

Step 2: Ask the employee his or her view of the issue. Listen and probe.
- Seek information by asking questions.
- Use open-ended questions that require employee input.
- Summarize the important points as you go.

Step 3: With the employee, find agreement on what needs to be accomplished.
- Ask the employee if you can agree on what is expected.
- Avoid forcing a solution on the employee.
- Agree on something, even if it's a basic principle or high-level expectation.

Step 4: Discuss alternatives for achieving success.
- Ask the employee for ideas to resolve the issue.
- Encourage the employee to suggest a solution he or she can support.
- Together, weigh the pros and cons of each alternative.

Step 5: Seek agreement on specific actions to be taken by you and the employee.
- Specify who, what, and when.
- Clarify your agreement by asking the employee what he or she will be doing.
- Restate your commitments to the employee.

Step 6: Express confidence in the employee's ability to resolve the issue and set a follow-up date.
- Be specific about your confidence.
- Be sincere.

Painless Performance Conversation Planner

Jumping right into a performance conversation without a little preparation can be painful. If you are nervous, concerned, or angry about the direction the performance conversation may take, it's even more important to stop and think things through. The painless performance conversation planner, shown below in Table 9.1 can help. The planner is a tool you will use to organize your thoughts. It follows the painless performance conversation model and asks thought-provoking questions to encourage you to think about what you will say at each step in the conversation.

Table 9.1 Painless Performance Conversation Planner

Discussion With: **Date/Time:**	
Step 1: Explain the situation ❖ What are the facts? ❖ What is the impact of the situation? ❖ Remember: Be concise!	
Step 2: Listen and probe ❖ What open-ended questions will you ask to encourage the employee to share his or her perspective? ❖ What reaction do you anticipate from the employee?	
Step 3: Find agreement ❖ What will you ask to define the change that needs to be made? ❖ What is a basic premise you and the employee can agree upon? ❖ How can you be sure not to force a solution on the employee?	
Step 4: Discuss alternatives ❖ What open-ended questions will you ask to encourage the employee to offer alternatives?	

(continued)

Table 9.1   (*continued*)

Discussion With: Date/Time:	
Step 5: Agree on next steps ❖ What open-ended questions will you ask to clarify your agreement with the employee?	
Step 6: Express confidence ❖ What will you say to convey your confidence in the employee's ability to address the issue?	

Painless Performance Conversation Planner

To use the planner, picture yourself across from the employee with whom you are planning to meet. Imagine the questions you will ask and the statements you will make. The questions on the left side of the planner will spur your thinking. On the right side of the planner, write the actual words you will use to move through each step of the model.

You don't have to script the entire conversation. However, it is helpful to write out the first sentence or two of each step so that you can clearly and confidently move the conversation forward. Once you have notes for each step in the model, you will have a better handle on how you lead the conversation.

Please note that the painless performance conversation planner should not be used during the actual conversation you have with the employee. Doing so sends a message to the employee that you have scripted the meeting and do not intend to fully hear the employee out. Instead, use the planner as a tool for your own preparation. Leave the completed planner in your desk during the conversation with the employee.

Reflection Question

In your next performance conversation, how can you use the painless performance conversation model and planner to prepare?

Completing the Planner

Table 9.2 is an example of what a completed planner might look like for our conversation with an employee named Brynn.

Painless Perspective

Have a plan for the meeting before you start. Otherwise, the conversation will not produce the results you have envisioned.

Table 9.2 Painless Performance Conversation Planner Sample

Discussion With: Date/Time:	Brynn January 17, 20XX/1:00 PM
Step 1: Explain the situation ❖ What are the facts? ❖ What is the impact of the situation? ❖ Remember: Be concise!	I've noticed that you've not submitted your client summary on time for the past three weeks. The report was two days late last week and four days late the week before. When the reports are submitted past the Friday deadline, the accounting team can't proceed with their work. What's going on?
Step 2: Listen and probe ❖ What open-ended questions will you ask to encourage the employee to share his or her perspective? ❖ What reaction do you anticipate from the employee?	What happened to cause the reports to be late? What is happening with your assignments that I should be aware of? Employee may be defensive or may want to avoid the issue.
Step 3: Find agreement ❖ What will you ask to define the change that needs to be made?	Can we agree that submitting the client summaries each Friday afternoon is critical to our operation? Can we agree that your client summaries are valuable to our operations?

(continued)

Table 9.2 (*continued*)

Discussion With:	Brynn
❖ What is a basic premise you and the employee can agree upon? ❖ How can you be sure not to force a solution on the employee?	
Step 4: Discuss alternatives ❖ What open-ended questions will you ask to encourage the employee to offer alternatives?	What ideas do you have to make sure the challenges you've had in the past few weeks don't continue to get in your way? What other barriers are you facing to getting your summaries submitted on time? What do you think you could do to address the challenge of preparing the summaries?
Step 5: Agree on next steps ❖ What open-ended questions will you ask clarify your agreement with the employee?	Let's summarize what we've come up with. You are going to . . . What other ideas do you have? What else do you have in mind?
Step 6: Express confidence ❖ What will you say to convey your confidence in the employee's ability to address the issue?	When you put your mind to something, you usually succeed. Let's meet in two weeks to see how things are going.

After completing the planner, the manager has a better idea about what he wishes to accomplish in the conversation with Brynn. He has anticipated Brynn's perspective and can confidently begin the conversation with a well-defined path.

In preparing for battle I have always found that plans are useless, but planning is indispensable.

—Dwight D. Eisenhower

Painless Performance Conversation Example

Here's an example of how the conversation with Brynn might sound once you've put all of the principles of a painless performance conversation in place.

In the manager's office or an otherwise private place without distractions, explain the situation and why the issue is important.

Manager: Hi, Brynn. I've noticed that you've not submitted your client summary on time for the past three weeks. The report was two days late last week and four days late the week before. When the reports are submitted past the Friday deadline, the accounting team can't proceed with their work. What's going on?

Ask the employee his or her view of the issue. Listen and probe.

Brynn: I didn't think it was a big deal. Last week I got caught up with some other details and the week before . . . I don't really remember. You know, I'm not the only one who drags a little bit when it comes to submitting those reports. I've noticed that Hudson is usually a day or two late, and no one has said anything to him.

Manager: We're talking about your performance now, and I want to make sure that we agree on the facts. Do we agree that your reports were submitted late for the past two weeks?

Brynn: Well, yes, but it really wasn't my fault. I had a training workshop scheduled one of the days and . . . Oh, I'll just make sure they're on time from now on.

Manager: What happened that caused them to be late?

Brynn: Oh, I don't know! I just need to get them done.

Manager: Something must have come up that kept you from getting them done.

Brynn: Well, two weeks ago I got tied up with the annual report team and then we got off on a tangent. Last week I took the afternoon off to spend time with my niece, who was in town visiting.

Manager: So each time, there's been a different reason?

Brynn: Yeah, the past few weeks have been really crazy.

With the employee, find agreement on what needs to be accomplished.

Manager: It has been a busy few weeks. Let's see where we are. Can we agree that submitting the client summaries each Friday afternoon is critical to our operation?

Brynn: Sure, but sometimes that's hard to do.

Discuss alternatives for achieving success.

Manager: I'm glad we agree on the deadline, and I see that sometimes Friday afternoon will be a tough time to be able to deliver a report. Let's talk about what gets in your way and how you're going to get the summaries turned in on time regardless of other things on your plate. What ideas do you have to make sure the challenges you've had in the past few weeks don't slow you down in the future?

Brynn: I don't know. I'll just make sure to get them done on time. I'll be careful not to schedule too much on Friday afternoons. Sometimes I book myself up with clients or meetings on Fridays, which doesn't leave me much time to get the paperwork done. I think I just lose track of time on those days.

Manager: That's a possibility. What else can you do to get the client summaries in on time?

Brynn: I don't know. Hmm . . .

Manager: How have you seen others on the team get the summaries done?

Brynn: Well, I know I need to have a plan each week so that I meet my numbers and have time to report them. I know Kristy does a great job with managing her time, and I need to do the same.

Manager: Okay, Kristy might have some suggestions for you. What other barriers are you facing to getting your summaries submitted on time?

Brynn: Well, to be honest, I'm not always excited about preparing those summaries. They can get pretty tedious, and I wonder if anyone ever looks at them.

Manager: I understand that preparing the client summaries may not seem directly relevant to the service you deliver. The summaries are important, however, to the accounting department, that uses your data to prepare invoices. Without your accurate summary, our billing would not be accurate. Your summaries lead straight to our bottom line. What other ideas do you have?

Brynn: I guess I could check with Kristy to find out if she has any tricks for getting the summaries completed. She seems to just crank them out, and I don't know how she does it.

Manager: That's a good idea. Kristy does seem to have mastered the art of preparing the weekly summaries. She might have some good tips for you. Anything else?

Brynn: Not that I can think of. This seems like a good start.

Seek agreement on specific actions to be taken by you and the employee.

Manager: Let's summarize what we've come up with. You are going to make sure that you get your client summaries submitted by the deadline each Friday, and you're going to be careful not too overbook yourself with client meetings or other commitments on those days. Next, you're going to talk to Kristy to see if she has any tips for easing the summary preparation process. Is that right?

Brynn: Sure. I'll go talk with Kristy today because I don't want to be late again.

Manager: I appreciate that, Brynn. What else do you have in mind?

Brynn: Nothing else. I'm really sorry. I'll make sure I'm a little more prompt from now on. I really didn't even know it was a big deal.

Express confidence in the employee's ability to resolve the issue and set a follow-up date.

Manager: I'm confident that this is not going to be an ongoing issue. When you put your mind to something, you do it. Let's meet in two weeks to see how things are going. How about meeting on the 29th at 1:30?

Brynn: That works for me. Thanks.

We are remembered for what we say (or don't say) and for how it was said.
—Jim Manton

In this example, the manager presented Brynn with the issue in a factual way and allowed Brynn to give her point of view. The manager remained focused on the desired outcome—timely reports—but allowed Brynn to explore what it will take to meet the expectation. In the end, Brynn owned the idea that the reports needed to be completed on Friday afternoon regardless of her other priorities.

Conversation Checkpoints

- The ideal location for a painless performance conversation is anywhere the manager and the employee can focus on the conversation.
- The ultimate goal of a painless performance conversation is to reinforce or help the employee change his or her behavior.
- Your state of mind will determine the outcome of the conversation.
- In a painless performance conversation, there are no surprises, the employee finds the solution, and the focus is on the future.
- The first conversation about a performance challenge will probably not be the last conversation. Plan to follow up.
- The painless performance conversation model and planner provide the road map for a productive meeting.

From the Field

From Larry, Police Lieutenant:

As a lieutenant I am responsible for supervising detectives who conduct investigations. Each new detective goes through an established training program. However, I have found that this training is effective only to a point.

I was assigned a newly promoted detective who was very motivated and eager to learn; however, his work product was poor and always late. Each report contained spelling and grammatical errors, and he sometimes left out important details. Soon, this detective was buried in a pile of administrative investigations and experiencing great stress. I could see fear in his eyes and a change in his personality. It was obvious that he was sinking in the paper storm.

One particular conversation seemed to turn the situation around. I began the conversation with a statement about what I'd been observing and then asked the detective a series of questions. The conversation went on for about an hour. As a result, we wrote a plan that included daily updates of his progress, training, and organizational tools like an online calendar and spell-checker.

The new system seemed to click with him, and he soon began to excel. During one of our weekly check-in meetings, he related to me that he felt good and was now in control of his cases.

Sound Bites from the Field

Here's how a portion of the conversation went between Larry and the detective:

Larry: I noticed that you seem overwhelmed with your caseload and have been submitting reports that contain errors. We've talked about the need to be timely and accurate with all of your paperwork. What's going on with you?

Detective: I'm just really having trouble right now keeping up with the workload. Sometimes I wonder if I'm not cut out for this job.

Larry: I believe you can do this, and I really want to see you succeed. What do you think you need to get a handle on things?

Detective: I don't know.

Larry: Tell me a little about what happens when you begin to get overwhelmed.

Detective: It seems like I can't wrap up the reports for one case before the next one comes in. I get partially done with a report and then get pulled to a new case before I can finish the last one. When I finally remember to get back to the first case, I'm so distracted that I can't remember the details. We are just so busy!

Larry: We have certainly been slammed lately. I'm unclear why you are moving on to a new case before you finish up the last one. Tell me more.

Detective: Well, I thought we were supposed to crank out as many as possible during a shift.

Larry: Yes, it's important that we close as many cases as possible, and every case requires a different amount of time to see it through. It seems to me that when you leave one case to work on another though, you aren't closing. Is that right?

Detective: Yeah. I'm trying to do as many as possible.

Larry: How do you think you could change things up a bit to be able to close more cases and do them more accurately?

Detective: If you are saying that I can slow down and not take as many cases, I could probably get these unfinished cases done.

Larry: How would slowing down impact your accuracy?

Detective: It would give me time to run a spell and grammar check at least.

Larry: Spell-checking is always a good idea, but fewer closed cases is not our goal. Eventually, you'll need to have the same or higher volume of closed cases. So what other ideas do you have for moving in that direction?

The conversation continued for over an hour, with Larry helping the detective explore alternatives for getting more cases closed and for completing them more accurately using technology that is available to officers. They met on a weekly basis, and after a few months, the detective was submitting higher-quality reports in a more timely manner.

Lessons Learned from the Field

Larry approached the detective with curiosity and a belief that improvement was possible. He was clear about his expectations for change and engaged the employee in a conversation about how the issues could be resolved. Although improvement of the employee's performance took time and patience, it resulted in a dedicated and productive employee.

Next Up

In Chapter 10 you'll explore the toughest performance conversations you may face. From influencing the performance of seasoned employees to addressing the office gossip, the next chapter will offer you more real-life examples of performance conversations that are painless.

10 | What If?

Your Toughest Performance Conversations

What if, at this very moment, I am living up to my full potential?

—Heidi Wagner

Throughout the previous chapters, you've learned the principles of painless performance conversations. From conveying your expectations to applying the four mind-sets, each chapter has provided specific skills and insights you can apply when facing a tough discussion. However, along the way you may have thought, "But what if . . .?" The purpose of this chapter is to answer some of the most common "what if" questions related to employee performance conversations. In this chapter you'll find sample conversation dialogue structured around the four mind-sets and the painless performance conversation model.

You'll explore common "what if" questions, including:

- **What if** the employee has been with the organization for many years and has received positive performance evaluations that are not accurate? Where do I start?
- **What if** the employee is entrenched in the old ways of doing business and is resistant to change?
- **What if** the employee spreads gossip and constantly stirs the pot?
- **What if** the employee has violated an important policy?
- **What if** the employee is struggling to keep up with the volume of work?
- **What if** I've been the manager for a while and have ignored certain performance issues, but I'm now ready to address an employee's poor performance?

Although each of these "what if" scenarios has a unique twist, the basic concepts of a painless performance conversation apply. Let's take a look at each one, consider the specific challenges, and apply the painless performance conversation model. Along the way, you'll see references to the four mind-sets and other painless principles.

Case Study—The Late Employee

What if the employee has been with the organization for many years and has received positive performance evaluations that are not accurate? Where do I start?

You have just inherited Heidi into your work group. She is a longtime employee who has a reputation for being somewhat unproductive. You have heard that Heidi is consistently late for work, often calls in sick on Mondays and Fridays, and rarely produces error-free work. Stories abound that Heidi has been heard being rude to customers on the phone.

When you take a look at the file left behind by previous managers, you find only glowing comments about Heidi. In fact, her last three performance evaluations are above average, and none of them mention attendance, accuracy, or rudeness. Heidi believes that she is a star performer.

You need to talk with Heidi about her most recent tardiness, which was this morning. You're afraid she will not be open to your concern since she has never received this kind of feedback before. However, ignoring the issues is only going to make the situation worse.

Commentary and Considerations

Because Heidi's previous performance evaluations do not mention past problems with attendance or accuracy, it's best to begin with a clean slate. As the new manager, your job is to first establish clear expectations for Heidi's performance, without blaming her for past behavior that you did not experience or that is not documented. Still, it's important to bring the most recent tardiness to her attention so that she has an opportunity to correct the behavior in the future.

Apply the questions from the Pet Peeve Formula to prepare for your conversation with Heidi:

- What exactly is the **behavior** that is not meeting your expectations?

    Heidi has arrived to work after the scheduled start time. The errors in her work and reported rudeness to customers will not be addressed in this conversation because there is no current evidence to support a discussion about these issues.

- How does the behavior **affect** the work environment, the organizational culture, others' work performance, or the employee's ability to meet job expectations?

    When Heidi is late, she is not available to serve customers. Her past performance evaluations are irrelevant to the current situation.

- What behavior do you **expect** to see instead?

    The expectation is that Heidi will arrive to work and be ready to serve customers at the scheduled start time. There is a gap between the expectation and Heidi's behavior.

Table 10.1 illustrates what the conversation between you and Heidi might sound like. Note the painless principles used throughout the conversation.

Conversation Example

Table 10.1   The Late Employee

Conversation Example	Painless Principles in Action
You: *Heidi, I noticed that today you arrived to work 15 minutes past your scheduled start time. What happened?*	Lead with behavior. Eliminate judgment.
Heidi: *Oh, I just woke up a little later this morning, and then I got stuck in traffic. Sorry about that.*	
You: *Is that all? Anything else going on?*	Listen and probe.
Heidi: *What's the big deal? I said I'd be on time from now on.*	
You: *We may not have talked about this during the short time that you've been in this department. This is a good time, however, to remind you that the expectation for attendance in this department is that you arrive on or before your scheduled start time and that you are ready to respond to customers when the doors open. Can we agree that promptness is important so that you can serve our customers?*	Reinforce your expectations.
Heidi *(a little frustrated):* *I told you it was a fluke. This morning I just slept in a little longer than usual.*	
You: *I understand that today was likely a one-time event. Going forward, can we agree that your arriving on time is critical to the department's ability to serve customers?*	Find agreement.
Heidi: *Well, I guess.*	
You: *Heidi, my goal is to support you here so that you can be successful. What do you need to meet this expectation?*	Inquire with purpose.
Heidi: *I just need to get up earlier.*	
You: *Is that all?*	Listen and probe.

(continued)

Table 10.1 *(continued)*

Conversation Example	Painless Principles in Action
Heidi: *Yeah. If I stay up too late watching television, it makes it hard to get out of bed in the morning. I just need to get to bed earlier.*	
You: *I can relate to that. If I'm up past 10:00 PM, it's hard to drag myself out of bed, too. Is there anything else you need to get here on time?*	Inquire with purpose.
Heidi: *No. I'll make sure I'm on time from now on.*	
You: *Okay. I know you will take care of it. We have a goal to be one of the highest-rated departments in the company. Our ability to serve customers promptly is key to that. I'm sure you'll do whatever you can to help with this.*	Reinforce your expectations. Express confidence.
Heidi: *Okay, thanks, and I'm sorry to have been late this morning.*	

Let's Apply It

Where would you start if you inherited an employee who has a history of positive performance evaluations, yet his or her performance is not meeting your expectations?

Case Study—The Resistant Employee

What if the employee is entrenched in the old ways of doing business and is resistant to change?

Julie, a veteran employee, is very opposed to the new system your organization has recently installed. She has stated her opposition to the new software loudly and clearly at staff meetings and in casual conversations.

The new system has been difficult to implement, but now that it is in use, you and the leadership team are convinced that it will save the organization time and money. Julie is a longtime employee who doesn't like change. You've seen her resist other changes in the past, and she has been particularly resistant to this new system.

Now that the system is up and running, you have gathered enough data to be certain that Julie is not using the new system and that she is discouraging others from using it, even though it is required of all employees. One team member told you that Julie said to him, "Just do it the old way. This system will die and go away soon enough."

Commentary and Considerations

The goal of your conversation with Julie will be to let her know you are concerned about her lack of support for the new system. You also want to find out what can be done to help Julie better utilize and support the system since it is here to stay. Your aim is to change her behaviors, rather than to convince her that the new system is a good one.

Apply the questions from the Pet Peeve Formula to prepare for your conversation with Julie:

- What exactly is the **behavior** that is not meeting your expectations?

  Julie is not using the new system, and she has told others not to use it.

- How does the behavior **affect** the work environment, the organizational culture, others' work performance, or the employee's ability to meet job expectations?

  When Julie does not use the new system, project costs are not accurately tracked.

- What behavior do you **expect** to see instead?

  Julie is expected to use the new system.

Table 10.2 illustrates what the conversation between you and Julie might sound like. Note the painless principles used throughout the conversation.

Conversation Example

Table 10.2   The Resistant Employee

Conversation Example	Painless Principles in Action
You: *Julie, lately I've noticed that you are not using the new system. I was also told that you have discouraged others on the team from using the system. The organization is committed to this new tool, and it is here to stay. Your support and full use of the system is critical to our success. What's going on?*	Lead with behavior. Eliminate judgment.
Julie: *That system is a piece of junk. I've worked here long enough to know that it's not going to last, and we'll be back to our old methods within the year.*	
You: *Why do you say that?*	Inquire with purpose.
Julie: *Because I've seen this before. New systems come and go. It's just easier to keep doing it the way I've done it for the past 20 years.*	
You: *Tell me why you believe this system is only temporary.*	Inquire with purpose.
Julie: *Because every other computer system we've implemented has failed. Why not this one?*	
You: *I believe this one is going to stay with us, considering the success we're having with it now. What else is keeping you from adopting the new tools available with this system?*	Reinforce your expectations. Inquire with purpose.
Julie: *Oh, I don't know. It's just so complicated, and it doesn't seem to make my life any easier. It's a real hassle.*	
You: *Can you give me an example?*	Inquire with purpose.
Julie: *Well, when I enter in my proposed project plan, which I know to be the best path, the computer always tells me to go a different way. So I just override the computer.*	

Table 10.2 (*continued*)

Conversation Example	Painless Principles in Action
You: *What else keeps you from fully utilizing the system?*	Inquire with purpose.
Julie: *That's about it. I just don't trust it.*	
You: *When we use the system, it allows us to track expenses and thus the cost of each project. As we become more cost-conscious and quality-focused as an organization, we need data to make the best decisions. When we don't use the system, we don't have that data. Can we agree that the new system has benefits that will make us more efficient and allow us to provide services in a more cost-effective manner?*	Find agreement.
Julie: *I don't know. It seems like a big waste of time and money to me.*	
You: *Can we agree that the system is probably not going away anytime soon, considering the success we've been having with it?*	Find agreement.
Julie: *Yeah, I'm afraid that's looking like the way it's going to be.*	
You: *Okay, if that's the case, what do you need to be able to support the system and use it to its full extent?*	Create a culture of ownership. Discuss alternatives.
Julie: *I don't know. I guess I just need to follow the project plan it gives me.*	
You: *That's a start, but I get the sense you are still not excited about this. What else needs to happen for you to fully utilize the new tool?*	Inquire with purpose.
Julie: *Well, you say that we get great data from it, but I don't see any of that. I just see the system as more work for me.*	

(*continued*)

Table 10.2 (*continued*)

Conversation Example	Painless Principles in Action
You: *So, seeing some of the financial reports would be helpful to you?*	Listen and probe.
Julie: *I know it's not critical to my job to have that information, but it might be helpful to see how my work, and the work of my coworkers, is feeding into something that you and the other managers use.*	
You: *That makes sense. We could share the weekly or monthly summary reports at the staff meeting.*	Agree on next steps.
Julie: *It might also be helpful if we got feedback on how we are contributing to the department's goals. I know that the department has set some measures for reducing costs, but we don't know how we're doing.*	
You: *Julie, that's a great idea. We need to do a better job of sharing the data with you and the team. That way you can see how your use of the system drives the results of our entire operation. We can certainly start to do that, beginning with Monday's staff meeting. Anything else?*	Agree on next steps. Inquire with purpose.
Julie: *No. I see that it's important to allow the system to track our project costs and guide our plans. It's just such a big change from the way we've always done things around here. I still like my paper and clipboard!*	
You: *I know it's tough to shift gears, especially when you've been committed to the organization for so long. I really appreciate your willingness to make the adjustment. From now on, I'll make sure you and the team are kept in the loop about how the data are used and about your progress. I know you will use the system and all its tools and encourage others to do so as well. Together, I think we can make this work.*	Express confidence.
Julie: *Me too.*	

Let's Apply It

How will you approach an employee who is entrenched in the old ways of doing business and resistant to change?

Case Study—The Gossip Who Stirs the Pot

What if the employee spreads gossip and constantly stirs the pot?

In his two years with the organization, Jack's work has always been accurate and on time. He also contributes new ideas for improving the work unit. Even though he gets his work done, Jack has a tendency to stir the pot. He engages in a lot of chitchat throughout the day with other members of the division and has been known to gossip about others and about management.

Today you were told by another staff member that Jack told her that management was going to do away with telecommuting. Telecommuting is a valued benefit that allows employees the opportunity to work at home one day per week. You know this rumor is not true, and you are not sure where Jack came up with this idea. Nevertheless, he seems to be spreading the idea among the staff members, and his gossip has become very disruptive. This rumor has distracted the team and affected morale. Usually you just ignore his gossiping because he gets his work completed and he is an informal leader in the group. This time he's gone too far.

Commentary and Considerations

The goal of your conversation will be to let Jack know you are concerned about his sharing information that has no legitimate basis. You also want to find out what can be done to help Jack contribute in a positive way, rather than in a disruptive way. Jack is not likely to stop gossiping altogether based on one conversation with you. However, you can make it clear that gossip is distracting to the work group and that you expect Jack to be a positive contributor to the work unit.

Apply the questions from the Pet Peeve Formula to prepare for your conversation with Jack:

- What exactly is the **behavior** that is not meeting your expectations?

    Jack told others that telecommuting is being discontinued when it is not.

- How does the behavior **affect** the work environment, the organizational culture, others' work performance, or the employee's ability to meet job expectations?

    When Jack tells others information that is not true, it is disruptive to the team, distracting others from their work.

- What behavior do you **expect** to see instead?

    Jack is expected to verify rumors before he shares them with others. He is also expected to positively affect others with his leadership skills.

Table 10.3 illustrates what the conversation between you and Jack might sound like. Note the painless principles used throughout the conversation.

Conversation Example

Table 10.3   The Gossip Who Stirs the Pot

Conversation Example	Painless Principles in Action
You: *Jack, today I heard you told several of your teammates that telecommuting was being eliminated. Because that is not true, I am concerned about where you got the information and that your sharing it with others is disruptive to our work environment. What's going on?*	Explain the situation. Lead with behavior.
Jack: *Oh, I heard that from one of the guys in IT. He seems to always be in the know. So it's not true?*	
You: *No, it's not true, and I'm concerned that your sharing a rumor with your colleagues distracts them from focusing on our important work. What was the purpose of sharing that information?*	Inquire with purpose.
Jack: *I just thought they'd like to know what I heard. I really thought the guy from IT was onto something. I can't believe he was wrong.*	

Table 10.3 (*continued*)

Conversation Example	Painless Principles in Action
You: *What else can you tell me about this rumor? I'm curious about how it started.*	Inquire with purpose.
Jack: *Oh, I don't know. Nothing else. We just talk.*	
You: *Can we agree that when you share false information or spread rumors it is a distraction to the team?*	Find agreement.
Jack: *I don't think it's that big of a deal.*	
You: *Can we agree that our work is intense and distractions only make it more difficult to achieve our goals?*	Find agreement.
Jack: *Well, sure. We do work in a pretty tension-filled environment.*	
You: *Okay. And can we agree that we need to work together to stay focused on reaching our targets?*	Find agreement.
Jack: *Yeah.*	
You: *Jack, you are one of our top performers. Others on the team look up to you and follow your lead. How can you make sure that you are positively influencing our work environment, rather than creating distractions?*	Discuss alternatives.
Jack: *What do you mean? I don't think I create distractions.*	
You: *As I said, you are an important part of this team and the rest of your colleagues look to you for leadership. I'd like to see you make the most of the influence you have. How do you feel about being seen as a leader?*	Reinforce your expectations.
Jack: *Well, I never really thought of myself as a leader.*	
You: *Your peers look up to you. What can you do to make sure you use that influence in a productive way?*	Discuss alternatives.

(*continued*)

Table 10.3   *(continued)*

Conversation Example	Painless Principles in Action
Jack: *Well, I guess I need to stop the water cooler chitchat.*	
You: *That's a good start, but I think there's more to it than that. What else?*	Inquire with purpose.
Jack: *I don't know. I didn't realize I was that influential around here.*	
You: *Jack, you are very influential with your peers. They respect what you have to say. I think you have an opportunity to help shape and guide this team in a positive direction if you put your mind to it. What do you think?*	Inquire with purpose.
Jack: *Well, I have noticed that they seem to listen to me. I guess I need to be a little more aware of what I say.*	
You: *You're a valuable member of this team, and I need your help to keep the group focused on our challenging goals. In the future, if you hear a rumor, come to me first. Together we can decide if it's the truth and, if so, how to share it with the others. We need to work together.*	Reinforce your expectations. Agree on next steps.
Jack: *That's cool. Oh, and I'm glad telecommuting is not going away. I love the one day each week I get to work from home!*	
You: *I'll make sure to let the team know the truth about this rumor and thanks for understanding how important it is to manage the flow of information to the team.*	Express confidence.

Let's Apply It

What will you consider the next time you talk with an employee about a behavior that is disruptive to the work unit?

People are generally better persuaded by the reasons which they have themselves discovered than by those which have come into the minds of others.

—Blaise Pascal

Case Study—Serious Policy Violations

What if the employee has violated an important policy?

Your organization has clear policies related to vehicle use while on company business. The policies state that employees should not talk on a cell phone while operating a company-owned vehicle. The policy, as well as state law, requires that seat belts be worn at all times. One of your inspectors, Bebe, drives a company-marked vehicle and is on the road 90 percent of her workday. Today you were driving down Sheldon Street on your way to an appointment, and you pulled up next to Bebe at a red light. She was on her personal cell phone, and you also noticed that she was not wearing her seat belt. She didn't notice you beside her at the intersection. You've never discussed these issues with Bebe before, but she did sign the organization's policy manual when she was hired.

Bebe needs to know that repeated violations of these policies will result in immediate disciplinary action. This is serious.

Commentary and Considerations

Even though this is the first time you and Bebe have discussed this issue, it is important that you make it clear that this is a serious rule violation that will result in disciplinary action should the behavior be repeated. Likewise, it's important to make space in the conversation to hear Bebe's perspective. This conversation has the potential to be a one-sided conversation. It is important to make sure Bebe has an opportunity to be listened to before you make your point.

Apply the questions from the Pet Peeve Formula to prepare for your conversation with Bebe:

- What exactly is the **behavior** that is not meeting your expectations?

    Bebe did not wear her safety belt while driving a company vehicle. She also used her cell phone while driving.

- How does the behavior **affect** the work environment, the organizational culture, others' work performance, or the employee's ability to meet job expectations?

    When Bebe doesn't fasten her safety belt and uses her cell phone while driving, she is putting herself at risk, as well as risking the safety of others. The behavior also creates a liability for the company.

- What behavior do you **expect** to see instead?

    Bebe is expected to wear her safety belt at all times when driving or riding in a company-owned vehicle. She is also expected to refrain from using the cell phone while driving.

Table 10.4 illustrates what the conversation between you and Bebe might sound like. Note the painless principles used throughout the conversation.

Conversation Example

Table 10.4   Serious Policy Violations

Conversation Example	Painless Principles in Action
You: *Bebe, earlier today I was driving down Sheldon and pulled up next to you. You were driving a company-marked vehicle.*	Explain the situation. Focus on evidence.
Bebe: *Really? I didn't even see you! I must have been into my music or something.*	
You: *Actually, when I pulled up beside you, you were on your cell phone, and I also noticed that you were not wearing your safety belt. Both are serious violations of policy. What was happening?*	Lead with behavior. Listen and probe.
Bebe: *Really? I'm sure I was wearing my seat belt, and I was probably just listening to a quick voicemail while at the stoplight.*	
You: *I am certain that you were not wearing your belt, and you were talking with someone on the cell phone. You were laughing and responding to whatever the person was saying.*	Lead with behavior. Focus on evidence.

Table 10.4 *(continued)*

Conversation Example	Painless Principles in Action
Bebe: *Oh, that must have been when I took a quick call from my son. He checks in with me when he gets home from school, and he was telling me about the A he got on his spelling test.*	
You: *It's important to be available to your family when they need you. It's also important to wear your seat belt and to refrain from using your cell phone while driving. In fact, both are serious violations that can result in disciplinary action.*	Reinforce your expectations.
Bebe: *Disciplinary action? Really? It was just one time.*	
You: *Since this is the first time we've discussed it, this conversation will be considered a verbal warning. The policies exist to ensure your safety and the safety of others. In the future, if you are found to be not wearing your safety belt or to be talking on the phone while driving, you will be subject to more severe disciplinary action. What do you need to do to make sure it doesn't get to that point?*	Discuss alternatives.
Bebe: *Well, I am certainly going to make sure I put on my seat belt before I begin driving. That's easy. As for the cell phone usage while driving, I'm not sure what I'm supposed to do if my son calls while I'm out on site visits. What am I supposed to do? Ignore his calls?*	
You: *As I said, it's important to be available to your family when they need you, and it's reasonable that you would take one short call in the afternoon to make sure he's gotten home okay. When you are driving and that call comes in, what are your options?*	Reinforce your expectations. Discuss alternatives.
Bebe: *Well, I guess I could let it go to voicemail and then check in with him when I get to my destination or back to the office.*	
You: *Okay. Any other ideas?*	Listen and probe.

(continued)

Table 10.4   (*continued*)

Conversation Example	Painless Principles in Action
Bebe: *I could pull over and take the call.*	
You: *Yes. That's a reasonable solution. Anything else?*	Listen and probe.
Bebe: *No. I think I know what I need to do. And I'm sorry you had to bring this up.*	
You: *I appreciate you being willing to find solutions, and I'm confident you'll be able to address these issues. Please let me know if there's anything I can do to help.*	Express confidence.
Bebe: *Okay. Thanks.*	

Let's Apply It

How will you address a major policy violation with an employee? How will you keep the conversation focused on the facts, rather than being distracted by the employee's emotion?

Case Study—The Struggling Employee

What if the employee is struggling to keep up with the volume of work?

Brian is a relatively new employee who has just completed training and has been assigned a caseload of his own. He appears to be dedicated and committed to getting the job done. However, today you received a call from a client who said he's been trying to reach Brian for a week. Brian has not responded to the client's e-mails and has not returned his calls.

Every time you observe Brian, he appears to be working. Today, you received the monthly summary report. Brian's production is at least 25 percent below that of his teammates and his case backlog has doubled in the past month.

Commentary and Considerations

In this case, the goal of the conversation is to help Brian identify strategies for addressing his increasing backlog. In addition, you want him to make a priority of getting back with customers, beginning with a return call to Mr. Lawson, the client who called to complain. You sense that Brian may not feel fully confident in his new job and that additional support and guidance may be necessary to help him work independently. Because he is still new to the job, you want to provide the resources he needs while not discouraging him.

Apply the questions from the Pet Peeve Formula to prepare for your conversation with Brian:

- What exactly is the **behavior** that is not meeting your expectations?

    Brian has not returned a client call, and his caseload has been increasing over the past month.
- How does the behavior **affect** the work environment, the organizational culture, others' work performance, or the employee's ability to meet job expectations?

    Clients are not being served, and the backlog of cases is increasing.
- What behavior do you **expect** to see instead?

    Brian is expected to return client calls within 24 hours of receipt. He is also expected to decrease the number of backlogged cases.

Table 10.5 illustrates what the conversation between you and Brian might sound like. Note the painless principles used throughout the conversation.

Conversation Example

Table 10.5   The Struggling Employee

Conversation Example	Painless Principles in Action
You: *Hi, Brian. I wanted to share with you the monthly summary report. It concerns me that your production is 25 percent below that of the rest of the team and your backlog has doubled. I also received a call from*	Explain the situation. Focus on the evidence.

(continued)

Table 10.5 (*continued*)

Conversation Example	Painless Principles in Action
Mr. Lawson, who said he left several messages for you that have not been returned. What's going on?	
Brian: *Mr. Lawson, huh? I'm just so busy with the file notes that I haven't had a chance to get back to him. I'll give him a call today.*	
You: *Tell me a little more about what's happening with your workload.*	Inquire with purpose.
Brian: *I guess I'm just learning. I'll do better next week, especially once these files are done.*	
You: *I know you've been putting in a lot of hours trying to keep up on your caseload. So what else is going on that leaves you with an increasing backlog?*	Listen and probe.
Brian: *Yeah, I know the backlog was supposed to go down when I came on board. I'm just overwhelmed with stuff right now.*	
You: *Overwhelmed? Tell me more.*	Listen and probe.
Brian: *Well, sometimes I'm not sure which steps to take when I get a complicated case. So I've put those cases aside and have been focusing on the ones I can crank out right away. I guess things have piled up.*	
You: *So some of the cases are really difficult for you?*	Listen and probe.
Brian: *Yeah, it sounded so easy in training, but some of these files are different from what we covered in class.*	
You: *My intent is to help you be successful, and our collective goal is to reduce the backlog and to be responsive to our clients. What do you need to be able to manage those more challenging files?*	Reinforce your expectations. Discuss alternatives.

Table 10.5   (*continued*)

Conversation Example	Painless Principles in Action
Brian: *I don't know. I'll just work harder.*	
You: *It may not be an issue of working harder bur rather providing you with extra support as you learn to work through the more complex cases. Would that be of interest?*	Discuss alternatives.
Brian: *Sure, what do you have in mind?*	
You: *I was going to ask you. What would be helpful at this point?*	Create a culture of ownership.
Brian: *Well, when I run into a tough case, it might be helpful to know whom I can turn to for help. I don't want to interrupt Tina, but I think she is probably the person who has the answers.*	
You: *I think Tina would be a good choice, and I know she's willing to help. If she's busy, what other options might you have?*	Discuss alternatives.
Brian: *I could check in with you.*	
You: *Yes, that's certainly an option, and I'm here to help. Anything else?*	Listen and probe.
Brian: *Knowing I have such a backlog now is pretty overwhelming. Sometimes I have trouble focusing with such a huge pile in front of me.*	
You: *What do you have in mind?*	Inquire with purpose.
Brian: *Well, maybe you could help me prioritize the cases and then we could see if someone else can help me with some of the most pressing ones. I think once I get caught up I will be better able to focus.*	
You: *We can try that. Let's sit down and talk about the specific cases tomorrow morning. Any other ideas?*	Agree on next steps.
Brian: *No. That should really help.*	

(*continued*)

Table 10.5   (*continued*)

Conversation Example	Painless Principles in Action
You: *Okay, so you are going to ask Tina or me for help when you hit a tough situation. Tomorrow we're going to go through your cases and prioritize the backlog. If possible I'll see if a few of these cases can be reassigned until you get caught up. Is that right?*	Agree on next steps.
Brian: *Yeah, that would be very helpful.*	
You: *Is there anything else you need at this point?*	Listen and probe.
Brian: *No, I think that will really help.*	
You: *Good. Tomorrow we'll take a look at that backlog and make a priority list, with returning Mr. Lawson's call as the first priority. Also, let's plan on getting together each Friday to review your progress and make adjustments as needed.*	Agree on next steps.
Brian: *Sounds good to me. I'll go call Mr. Lawson right now. See you in the morning.*	

Let's Apply It

What is your approach when an employee is struggling to keep up with the volume of work? How can you best support the employee?

Case Study—The Longterm Employee

What if I've been the manager for a while and have ignored certain performance issues, but I'm now ready to address an employee's poor performance?

You've been managing the same group of employees for at least three years. You've had a few staff members come and go, but mostly it's the same individuals you started with. When you started as the manager of this work group, you were new to the organization and still learning the ropes. Because you were new and overwhelmed, you did not establish clear expectations for performance. As time has passed, you've been so busy putting out fires and meeting deadlines that you haven't taken the time to be clear about what you really expect of your team. As a result, you have a few superstars and a few slackers on the team.

You sense that the star performers are beginning to get frustrated by the poor performance of a few. In particular, Marilyn is your weak link. She has been with the organization longer than anyone else, and her work product is barely adequate. She often arrives late and does not assist her teammates when they need help. For quite a while, she has submitted work that contains errors and important omissions. You know you need to begin addressing these issues before your strong performers choose to leave.

Commentary and Considerations

It's easy to pile multiple concerns onto an employee when you haven't said anything over time. Resist the urge to air all of your grievances with Marilyn at once. Lead the conversation with the behaviors you have seen most recently and the results those behaviors have on the work group. For example, you can provide evidence of reports that include errors. You can also mention the most recent examples of tardiness. It will be important to be clear about your expectations while allowing Marilyn space in the conversation to consider your message. Remember that it's not likely that Marilyn will resolve all of your concerns after one conversation. Be prepared for additional discussions to reinforce your expectations.

Apply the questions from the Pet Peeve Formula to prepare for your conversation with Marilyn:

- What exactly is the **behavior** that is not meeting your expectations?

  Marilyn has submitted work with omissions and errors. She also arrives to work 30 to 45 minutes after the rest of the team.

- How does the behavior **affect** the work environment, the organizational culture, others' work performance, or the employee's ability to meet job expectations?

  When Marilyn submits reports with omissions or errors, the team is unable to accurately account for its costs. When she arrives later than the rest of the team, expectations are inconsistently applied, which affects team morale.

- What behavior do you **expect** to see instead?

    Marilyn is expected to arrive to work by 8:30 AM each day. She is also expected to list all of her projects in the work order summary to accurately account for her time.

Table 10.6 illustrates what the conversation between you and Marilyn might sound like. Note the painless principles used throughout the conversation.

Conversation Example
Table 10.6   The Longterm Employee

Conversation Example	Painless Principles in Action
You: *I realize this may come as a surprise after our three years of working together, and I believe I owe it to you to share what I'm seeing. I've noticed that you are consistently coming into the office 30 to 45 minutes after the rest of the team. I've also noticed that the work order summaries you've prepared, at least those submitted in the past month, have not included all of the jobs you've worked on. I'm concerned because you are a senior member of this team and looked on by the others as a role model. What's up?*	Lead with behavior. Focus on the evidence.
Marilyn: *I don't know what you mean. I'm not doing anything differently from what I've done for the past 15 years.*	
You: *I realize this may be new information for you and that I should have said something sooner. At this point, I owe it to you to bring it to your attention. I'm concerned about your work.*	
Marilyn: *Why is this a problem now?*	
You: *When I began looking at it, I realized we have some big inconsistencies, and your work stood out to me. In particular, your start time and your work order summaries are of concern.*	

Table 10.6 (*continued*)

Conversation Example	Painless Principles in Action
Marilyn: *So what do you want me to do about it?*	
You: *Well, to begin with, can we agree on a few standards? For example, can we agree that the team begins work at 8:30 AM?*	Find agreement.
Marilyn: *We've never had an official start time before. It's always been pretty flexible around here.*	
You: *I realize that our official start time has never been explicitly stated. However, it needs to be clear so that everyone knows what's expected. Can we agree that it's important for you to be here at 8:30 AM to join the rest of the team?*	Reinforce your expectations. Find agreement.
Marilyn: *I guess so. Although I'm not sure I understand what the big deal is.*	
You: *Our work group is continuing to grow and change. Part of that shift requires us to be clear about our expectations of one another. When we are all on the same page, it allows us to focus on the work at hand. Can we agree that 8:30 AM is a reasonable start time?*	Reinforce your expectations. Find agreement.
Marilyn: *Sure . . . and what was your issue with my reports?*	
You: *Since our group is under greater scrutiny to account for its costs, the weekly reports are more important than ever. I noticed that you have completed jobs, which have not made it into your reports. For example, two weeks ago you worked on a project for Accounts Payable, yet I didn't see it referenced on your weekly summary. When you don't list all of your projects, we are unable to account for all of our costs and your time.*	Focus on the evidence.
Marilyn: *This is the first I've heard that anyone pays attention to those reports. We've been doing them for years, and no one has ever said a thing.*	

(*continued*)

Table 10.6 (*continued*)

Conversation Example	Painless Principles in Action
You: *I know we haven't taken the cost reports seriously in the past, but with the increased pressure on us to balance our expenses with our output, the reports are more important than ever before.*	Reinforce your expectations.
Marilyn: *So why are you bringing this up to me? Why not talk to the whole group? I know I'm not the only one to fudge on those forms in order to get them in on time.*	
You: *I intend to ask the entire staff how we can better utilize the forms to track our work orders. Your omissions are the most obvious to me, though. What can you do to make sure they are more accurate?*	Create a culture of ownership. Inquire with purpose.
Marilyn: *I don't know. I guess I'll just do a better job of tracking each project.*	
You: *Is that all?*	Listen and probe.
Marilyn: *I used to keep a logbook with me at all times to keep track of that time. For some reason, I don't do it any more.*	
You: *That's an idea. What else?*	Listen and probe.
Marilyn: *I wonder how the others on the team keep track of their project work?*	
You: *Good question. I'm thinking we should talk about this at our next staff meeting to compare best practices.*	Agree on next steps.
Marilyn: *That would be helpful.*	
You: *Anything else?*	Listen and probe.
Marilyn: *Not that I can think of.*	
You: *Okay. Let's summarize what we've discussed. You agree to arrive by 8:30 AM each morning so that the entire team can begin at the same time.*	Agree on next steps.

Table 10.6 (*continued*)

Conversation Example	Painless Principles in Action
Marilyn: *Yep.*	
You: *And you're going to keep a more accurate accounting of your project time so that your weekly work order report is accurate. This is more important now than before because of the increased scrutiny we are facing.*	Agree on next steps.
Marilyn: *Yeah. I don't like doing it, but I can see why it's important.*	
You: *Marilyn, your years of experience and your perspective are valuable to this group. I count on you to be a model for the rest of the team. What else can I do to support you?*	Express confidence. Inquire with purpose.
Marilyn: *I don't know. Just let me know what you need from me, I guess.*	
You: *You can bet I will. In fact, why don't we plan on meeting regularly to discuss how things are going and to find ways you can support and participate in the new directions we are taking? How does that sound?*	Agree on next steps.
Marilyn: *Fine with me.*	
You: *Let's reconnect a week from Friday to touch base and see how things are going. Thanks for your time today.*	

Let's Apply It

What performance issues have you ignored? What is the impact on the team? What do you need to do to begin to shift the performance of certain team members?

Reflection Questions

What is your "what if" question? What situation are you facing now where a painless performance conversation is needed? What principles can you use to help you lead the conversation to a positive outcome?

Next Up

Now that you have made it through all 10 chapters, please explore the additional resources provided on our website www.painlessperformance conversations.com.

At this site, you will find additional resources that will support your continuing efforts to lead painless performance conversations.

Conclusion

For most managers, performance conversations do not come easy. They require preparation, confidence, and a clear understanding of what you are trying to accomplish. This book was written to give you the practical perspective and the "here's how you say it" tools so that you can tackle performance conversations with confidence. I have a few final thoughts to share before you head off to take on the next performance conversation. They are not necessarily the nuts and bolts of the conversation, but they are the heart and soul. May these concluding thoughts support you as you embark on the important conversations that will positively affect your employees and your organization.

If Not You, Then Who?

When it comes to helping an employee enhance his or her performance, there's no one else who has that direct responsibility. It's you and only you. Some managers think it would be nice to delegate the people stuff, but that's your job. If you are expecting something other than what you are getting from an employee, you are the best person to raise the issue. Do not pass the employee performance buck.

Develop Your Craft

Feeling confident in your role as a manager takes practice. Confidence is built over time. Take little steps each day to practice having performance conversations. Separate attitudes from behaviors and focus on providing specific feedback related to the behaviors you observe. Each week, reflect on the challenges you've taken on and the tools that worked for you. Little by little, you'll build confidence as you become more proficient. No one is born an expert at leading performance conversations. It's a skill you hone over time. Remember, you're a work in progress.

Model Successful People to Be One

One of the best ways to learn how to manage performance is to model your behaviors after others you admire. Look around your organization and find managers who are successful. Which managers appear to be confidently managing the performance of their work groups? Who is seeing the greatest amount of success? Watch how they deliver the tough messages. Listen to the questions they ask. Model your approach after those you look up to.

Practice Visualization

Elite athletes and A-list actors use visualization to prepare for their most memorable performances. Leading a performance conversation is not much different. Before you enter into your next performance conversation, use the painless performance conversation planner to imagine yourself confidently and successfully leading the discussion. Visualizing yourself across from the employee, asking open-ended questions, prepares you for the real event. Even if you don't write out a plan using the planner, just thinking about the steps you'd like to follow will boost your confidence once the actual conversation is under way.

Focus, Focus, Focus

To affect performance, you have to be clear about what you are trying to accomplish. Babies have intense focus when you show them a shiny object. They can't take their eyes off of it. Your vision for the outcome of the conversation is like a shiny object. Don't let yourself get derailed by irrelevant side issues or excuses that won't improve the situation. Focus on the task at hand and continually bring the conversation back to your goal, which is to help the employee be successful.

Mind Your Negative Thoughts

We all fight the voice in our head that tells us this is going to be difficult. That voice might tell you, "Oh, you don't want to have this conversation," or "Why don't you just wait and see if the employee changes?" These thoughts do nothing but slow you down. They aren't helpful and do nothing to build your confidence. When you begin to hear the negative voice in your head, replace it with positive self-talk. Telling yourself that leading this conversation is your obligation and reminding yourself that you are helping the employee and the organization by initiating the discussion are more positive messages.

Begin with the Hardest Conversation

Some performance conversations are harder than others. The longer you put them off, the harder they become. By procrastinating, you may also unintentionally dilute the importance of the issue in the employee's eyes. The longer you wait, the harder it will be. Build your confidence by tackling the toughest issue today. The sooner you address the issue, the sooner the employee can begin making improvements. What conversation is waiting to begin?

Wait through the Silence

In tough conversations, there's a lot going on in the minds of everyone involved. Because emotions are competing for space in your brain, a little silence can provide the necessary space for everyone to think. Stop talking and wait to hear what the employee has to say. If the employee is not saying much, ask another question and wait for a response. The more patient you are, the more space you'll create for the employee to share their perspective. The more you hear from the employee, the more you'll understand and the more he or she will own the ultimate solution.

Shift Your Focus

We often enter performance conversations with the goal of fixing something. Many times, there is no fix for the issue; rather, a shift in perspective is in order. Before you enter your next performance conversation, consider these shifts:

- Focus on what's right, not what's wrong.
- Focus on what you have, not what you don't have.
- Focus on solutions, not problems.

Ask for Reassurance

Sometimes we need a little boost from one another. Managing employees can be an overwhelming task, and it can be lonesome. Don't be afraid to ask someone close to you for reassurance before you dive into the tough conversations. Your boss, a colleague, a representative from human resources, an executive coach—all of these individuals can be a sounding board to remind you that you are doing the right thing by having the conversation. Once you talk it through with a neutral party, the problems don't seem so big.

Have Patience

Finally, remember that the initial conversation is just the beginning and that you may not see dramatic changes from one conversation. Behavior change and eventual shifts in attitude take time. The first conversation may not go the way you have envisioned. That's okay. Learn from each encounter and try again. Even if the conversation doesn't result in the immediate changes you envisioned, you have had an impact. Be patient and keep at it.

Taking on the tough issues that come up in the workplace doesn't have to be impossible. With the right tools and the right frame of mind, you can positively influence the performance of others.

Appendix

Tools for Painless Performance Conversations

You've just been introduced to numerous tips and ideas for confidently leading performance conversations. This section includes the most popular, widely-used tools that you will reference again and again.

Agenda for an Expectation-Setting Conversation

1. State the purpose of the conversation.
   - To establish clear expectations for performance
   - To define what success looks like
   - To ensure the employee can thrive in his or her role
2. Review critical organizational expectations.
   - Share copies of the organization's mission, vision, and/or values.
   - Explain how your work group supports these organizational expectations.
   - Show the employee how his or her work supports the organization's goals.
   - Remind the employee about how his or her contribution, on a daily basis, matters.
3. Review your list of expectations.
   - Share a written copy of your list with the employee. Give the employee a copy of your list to keep.
   - Review each item on the list in detail.
   - Ask the employee if he or she has questions about the list or if there is anything he or she would like to add.
   - Make necessary changes to your list of expectations based on the employee's feedback.
4. Ask the employee what he or she needs. Engage the employee in a dialogue about the expectations you have set forth. Ask questions, such as:
   - What do you need to meet the organizational expectations?
   - What expectation will be the most challenging for you?
   - What do you need to meet the expectations on the list?
   - What concerns do you have about the definition of success that has been shared with you?
   - How can I help you meet these expectations?

- What obstacles do you anticipate?
- What expectations do you have for this job?
- What expectations do you have of me, your manager?

5. Express confidence.
   - Tell the employee that your goal is to help him or her be successful.
   - Encourage the employee to come to you with questions or concerns.
   - Express your confidence in the employee's ability to be successful.

Agenda for a Painless Performance Conversation

Step 1. Explain the situation and why the issue is important.
- State the facts.
- Explain the impact of the situation on the organization.
- Be concise!

Step 2. Ask the employee his or her view of the issue. Listen and probe.
- Seek information by asking questions.
- Use open-ended questions that require employee input.
- Summarize the important points as you go.

Step 3. With the employee, find agreement on what needs to be accomplished.
- Ask the employee if you can agree on what is expected.
- Avoid forcing a solution on the employee.
- Agree on something, even if it's a basic principle or high-level expectation.

Step 4. Discuss alternatives for achieving success.
- Ask the employee for ideas to resolve the issue.
- Encourage the employee to suggest a solution he or she can support.
- Together, weigh the pros and cons of each alternative.

Step 5. Seek agreement on specific actions to be taken by you and the employee.
- Specify who, what, and when.
- Clarify your agreement by asking the employee what he or she will be doing.
- Restate your commitments to the employee.

Step 6. Express confidence in the employee's ability to resolve the issue and set a follow-up date.

- Be specific about your confidence.
- Be sincere.

Painless Performance Conversation Planner

Discussion With: **Date/Time:**	
Step 1: Explain the situation. ❖ What are the facts? ❖ What is the impact of the situation? ❖ Remember: Be concise!	
Step 2: Listen and probe. ❖ What open-ended questions will you ask to encourage the employee to share his or her perspective? ❖ What reaction do you anticipate from the employee?	
Step 3: Find agreement. ❖ What will you ask to define the change that needs to be made? ❖ What is a basic premise you and the employee can agree upon? ❖ How can you be sure not to force a solution on the employee?	
Step 4: Discuss alternatives. ❖ What open-ended questions will you ask to encourage the employee to offer alternatives?	
Step 5: Agree on next steps. ❖ What open-ended questions will you ask to clarify your agreement with the employee?	
Step 6: Express confidence. ❖ What will you say to convey your confidence in the employee's ability to address the issue?	

About the Management Education Group, Inc.

The Management Education Group, Inc., is dedicated to helping leaders develop the confidence they need to painlessly manage employee performance. Service offerings include:

- **Workshops**—*fast-paced, practical, real life*

  Our workshops boost leader confidence and create engagement in the workplace by supporting a painless approach to employee performance management.

- **Consulting**—*performance-driven, outcome-focused, transformational*

  We can help your organization design a customized employee performance management system that establishes clear performance expectations for employees, links employee performance to overall organizational objectives, encourages frequent dialogue about performance between managers and employees, and allows for recognition of top performers.

- **Books**—*tools, support, engagement*

  Marnie Green's books have supported leaders worldwide, providing the practical resource every manager needs to confidently support the performance of his or her employees.

- **Webinars**—*entertaining, powerful, useful*

  Marnie Green's webinars, live and recorded, draw large crowds because they provide a shot in the arm for leaders who want to positively affect employee performance.

To contact the Management Education Group, visit www.ManagementEducationGroup.com or call 480-705-9394.

About the Author

Marnie E. Green, Principal Consultant of the Management Education Group, Inc., is the nation's go-to expert in the development of public sector leaders. She has spent the past 25 years providing valuable step-by-step programs and facilitation services that create more confident government leaders. Along the way she has served as an executive coach to local leaders at the highest levels.

Green is the author of the award-winning *Painless Performance Evaluations: A Practical Approach to Managing Day-to-Day Employee Performance*.

Her consulting and training clients include public agencies from coast to coast, including the US Bureau of Land Management; the states of Alaska, Arizona, and Montana; the county of San Diego, California; the cities of Phoenix, Las Vegas, San Jose, and Honolulu; and various special districts and authorities, including Phoenix-Mesa Gateway Airport, Salt River Project, and West Basin Municipal Water District.

Green holds a bachelor's degree in Personnel Management and a master's degree in Business Administration, Finance, both from Arizona State University. She is a graduate of Harvard University, Kennedy School of Government's Art and Practice of Leadership Development residency program.

Active in several professional associations, Green is a member of the Society for Human Resource Management and the National Speakers Association and has served on numerous boards and committees for the International Public Management Association for Human Resources. She is a frequent speaker at local, national, and international conferences on workforce-related issues, including leadership development, recruiting and retaining top talent, the workforce of the future, and employee performance management.

She doesn't like to sit still. In addition to serving organizations worldwide, her personal accomplishments include reaching the top of Africa's highest peak, Mount Kilimanjaro; circumnavigating western Europe's highest mountain, Mount Blanc; riding portions of the Tour de France; and volcano boarding in Nicaragua.

To learn more about Green, go to www.marniegreen.com.

http://www.facebook.com/ManagementEducationGroup

http://www.linkedin.com/in/marniegreen

http://www.twitter.com/MarnieGreen

Index